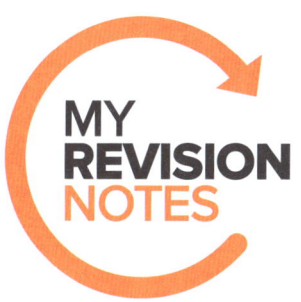

Cambridge National

Level 1/Level 2

SPORT SCIENCE
SECOND EDITION

For the J828 specification

Sue Young

Symond Burrows

Photo credits

page 11 © Dusan Kostic / stock.adobe.com; **page 12** © Cultura Allies / stock.adobe.com; **page 13** © JackF / stock.adobe.com; **page 14** © Rawpixel.com / stock.adobe.com; **page 15** (top) © Shakzu / stock.adobe.com; **page 15** (bottom) © Kara / stock.adobe.com; **page 16** © haizon / stock.adobe.com; **page 17** © mRGB / stock.adobe.com; **page 18** (top) © Maridav / stock.adobe.com; **page 18** (bottom) © Corepics VOF / Shutterstock.com; **page 20** © Bit24 / stock.adobe.com; **page 22** © Simon Balson / Alamy Stock Photo; **page 24** © Lawrence Wee / Shutterstock.com; **page 26** © Jules Frazier / Photodisc / Getty Images; **page 27** (top) © Maridav / stock.adobe.com; **page 27** (bottom) © Cpl. Chelsea Flowers Anderson / U.S. Marine Corps / PJF Military Collection / Alamy Stock Photo; **page 29** © StratfordProductions / stock.adobe.com; **page 30** © Rawpixel.com / Shutterstock.com; **page 33** © Liza5450 / stock.adobe.com; **page 37** © Martin81 / Shutterstock; **page 38** © ZUMA Press, Inc. / Alamy Stock Photo; **page 51** © OZMedia / stock.adobe.com; **page 53** (top) © Photographee.eu / stock.adobe.com; **page 53** (middle) © Microgen / stock.adobe.com; **page 53** (bottom) © Kimberly Reinick / stock.adobe.com; **page 56** © Rich Graessle / Icon Sportswire / Corbis / Getty Images; **page 57** © Andrej Chalupník / Alamy Stock Photo; **page 58** © Andrey Popov / stock.adobe.com; **page 60** © Cindy Yamanaka / Orange County Register / MCT / Sipa USA / Alamy Stock Photo; **page 62** © Witsawat / stock.adobe.com

Every effort has been made to trace all copyright holders, but if any have been inadvertently overlooked, the Publishers will be pleased to make the necessary arrangements at the first opportunity.

Although every effort has been made to ensure that website addresses are correct at time of going to press, Hodder Education cannot be held responsible for the content of any website mentioned in this book. It is sometimes possible to find a relocated web page by typing in the address of the home page for a website in the URL window of your browser.

Hachette UK's policy is to use papers that are natural, renewable and recyclable products and made from wood grown in well-managed forests and other controlled sources. The logging and manufacturing processes are expected to conform to the environmental regulations of the country of origin.

Orders: please contact Hachette UK Distribution, Hely Hutchinson Centre, Milton Road, Didcot, Oxfordshire, OX11 7HH. Telephone: +44 (0)1235 827827. Email education@hachette.co.uk. Lines are open from 9 a.m. to 5 p.m., Monday to Friday. You can also order through our website: www.hoddereducation.co.uk

ISBN: 978 1 3983 5116 5

© Sue Young and Symond Burrows 2022

First published in 2020
This edition published in 2022 by
Hodder Education,
An Hachette UK Company
Carmelite House
50 Victoria Embankment
London EC4Y 0DZ

www.hoddereducation.co.uk

Impression number   10 9 8 7 6 5 4

Year   2025

All rights reserved. Apart from any use permitted under UK copyright law, no part of this publication may be reproduced or transmitted in any form or by any means, electronic or mechanical, including photocopying and recording, or held within any information storage and retrieval system, without permission in writing from the publisher or under licence from the Copyright Licensing Agency Limited. Further details of such licences (for reprographic reproduction) may be obtained from the Copyright Licensing Agency Limited, www.cla.co.uk

Cover photo: © vladakela – stock.adobe.com

Typeset in India

Printed and bound in Great Britain by Bell and Bain Ltd, Glasgow

A catalogue record for this title is available from the British Library.

Get the most from this book

This book will help you to revise for your Cambridge National in Sport Science exam (Unit R180 Reducing the risk of sports injuries and dealing with common medical conditions). You can find out more about the exam on pages 7–10.

Everyone has to decide his or her own revision strategy, but it is essential to review your work, learn it and test your understanding. These Revision Notes will help you to do that in a planned way, topic by topic. Use this book as the cornerstone of your revision and don't hesitate to write in it: personalise your notes and check your progress by ticking off each section as you revise.

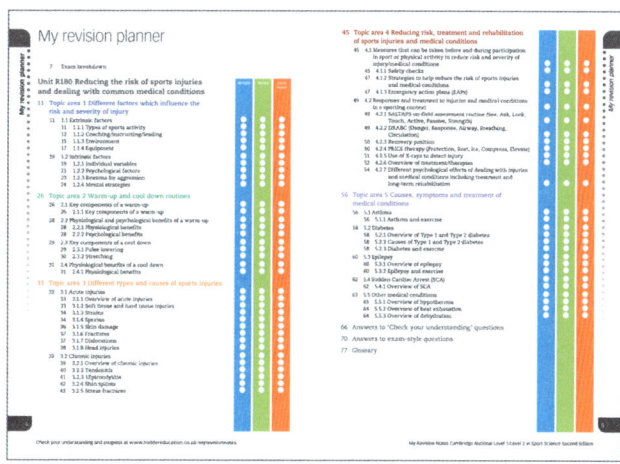

Tick to track your progress

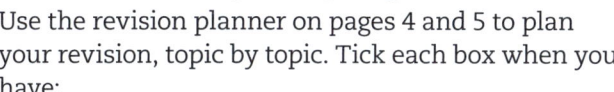

Use the revision planner on pages 4 and 5 to plan your revision, topic by topic. Tick each box when you have:
+ revised and understood a topic
+ tested yourself
+ practised exam questions.

You can also keep track of your revision by ticking off each topic heading in the book. You may find it helpful to add your own notes as you work through each topic.

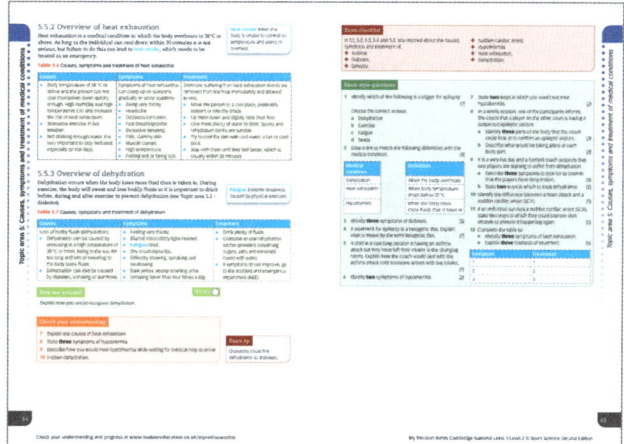

Features to help you succeed

Exam tips

Expert tips to help you polish your exam technique and maximise your chances in the exam.

Typical mistakes

Common mistakes made by other students and guidance on how to avoid them.

Check your understanding

Short questions to test your knowledge and understanding as you work through the course. Answers are given at the back of the book.

Now test yourself

Revision activities to guide your note-taking.

Definitions and key words

Clear, concise definitions of essential-to-know terms.

Exam-style questions

Practice exam questions. Use them to consolidate your revision and practise your exam skills. Answers are given at the back of the book.

My Revision Notes Cambridge National Level 1/Level 2 in Sport Science Second Edition

My revision planner

7 Exam breakdown

Unit R180 Reducing the risk of sports injuries and dealing with common medical conditions

11 Topic area 1: Different factors which influence the risk and severity of injury

- 11 1.1 Extrinsic factors
  - 11 1.1.1 Types of sports activity
  - 12 1.1.2 Coaching/instructing/leading
  - 15 1.1.3 Environment
  - 17 1.1.4 Equipment
- 19 1.2 Intrinsic factors
  - 19 1.2.1 Individual variables
  - 21 1.2.2 Psychological factors
  - 23 1.2.3 Reasons for aggression
  - 24 1.2.4 Mental strategies

26 Topic area 2: Warm-up and cool down routines

- 26 2.1 Key components of a warm-up
  - 26 2.1.1 Key components of a warm-up
- 28 2.2 Physiological and psychological benefits of a warm-up
  - 28 2.2.1 Physiological benefits
  - 28 2.2.2 Psychological benefits
- 29 2.3 Key components of a cool down
  - 29 2.3.1 Pulse lowering
  - 30 2.3.2 Stretching
- 31 2.4 Physiological benefits of a cool down
  - 31 2.4.1 Physiological benefits

33 Topic area 3: Different types and causes of sports injuries

- 33 3.1 Acute injuries
  - 33 3.1.1 Overview of acute injuries
  - 33 3.1.2 Soft tissue and hard tissue injuries
  - 34 3.1.3 Strains
  - 34 3.1.4 Sprains
  - 36 3.1.5 Skin damage
  - 37 3.1.6 Fractures
  - 37 3.1.7 Dislocations
  - 38 3.1.8 Head injuries
- 39 3.2 Chronic injuries
  - 39 3.2.1 Overview of chronic injuries
  - 40 3.2.2 Tendonitis
  - 41 3.2.3 Epicondylitis
  - 42 3.2.4 Shin splints
  - 43 3.2.5 Stress fractures

Check your understanding and progress at www.hoddereducation.co.uk/myrevisionnotes

45 Topic area 4: Reducing risk, treatment and rehabilitation of sports injuries and medical conditions

- 45   4.1 Measures that can be taken before and during participation in sport or physical activity to reduce risk and severity of injury/medical conditions
  - 45   4.1.1 Safety checks
  - 47   4.1.2 Strategies to help reduce the risk of sports injuries and medical conditions
  - 47   4.1.3 Emergency action plans (EAPs)
- 49   4.2 Responses and treatment to injuries and medical conditions in a sporting context
  - 49   4.2.1 SALTAPS on-field assessment routine (See, Ask, Look, Touch, Active, Passive, Strength)
  - 49   4.2.2 DRABC (Danger, Response, Airway, Breathing, Circulation)
  - 50   4.2.3 Recovery position
  - 50   4.2.4 PRICE therapy (Protection, Rest, Ice, Compress, Elevate)
  - 51   4.2.5 Use of X-rays to detect injury
  - 52   4.2.6 Overview of treatment/therapies
  - 54   4.2.7 Different psychological effects of dealing with injuries and medical conditions including treatment and long-term rehabilitation

56 Topic area 5: Causes, symptoms and treatment of medical conditions

- 56   5.1 Asthma
  - 56   5.1.1 Asthma and exercise
- 58   5.2 Diabetes
  - 58   5.2.1 Overview of Type 1 and Type 2 diabetes
  - 58   5.2.2 Causes of Type 1 and Type 2 diabetes
  - 58   5.2.3 Diabetes and exercise
- 60   5.3 Epilepsy
  - 60   5.3.1 Overview of epilepsy
  - 60   5.3.2 Epilepsy and exercise
- 62   5.4 Sudden Cardiac Arrest (SCA)
  - 62   5.4.1 Overview of SCA
- 63   5.5 Other medical conditions
  - 63   5.5.1 Overview of hypothermia
  - 64   5.5.2 Overview of heat exhaustion
  - 64   5.5.3 Overview of dehydration

66 Answers to 'Check your understanding' questions

70 Answers to exam-style questions

76 Glossary

My revision planner

Countdown to my exam

6–8 weeks to go

- Start by looking at the specification – make sure you know exactly what material you need to revise and the style of the examination. Use the revision planner on pages xx and xx to familiarise yourself with the topics.
- Organise your notes, making sure you have covered everything on the specification. The revision planner will help you to group your notes into topics.
- Work out a realistic revision plan that will allow you time for relaxation. Set aside days and times for all the subjects that you need to study, and stick to your timetable.
- Set yourself sensible targets. Break your revision down into focused sessions of around 40 minutes, divided by breaks. These Revision Notes organise the basic facts into short, memorable sections to make revising easier.

REVISED

4–6 weeks to go

- Read through the relevant sections of this book and refer to the 'remember' tips, key terms, summaries and exam skills. Tick off the topics as you feel confident about them. Highlight those topics you find difficult and look at them again in detail.
- Test your understanding of each topic by working through the 'Now test yourself' questions in the book. Look up the answers at the back of the book.
- Make a note of any problem areas as you revise, and ask your teacher to go over these in class.
- Look at past papers. They are one of the best ways to revise and practise your exam skills. Write or prepare planned answers to the exam practice questions provided in this book. Check your answers at the back of the book or online at **www.hoddereducation.co.uk/myrevisionnotesdownloads**
- Try using different revision methods as you work through the sections. For example, you can make notes using mind maps, spider diagrams or flash cards.
- Track your progress using the revision planner and give yourself a reward when you have achieved your target.

REVISED

One week to go

- Try to fit in at least one more timed practice of an entire past paper and seek feedback from your teacher, comparing your work closely with the mark scheme.
- Check the revision planner to make sure you haven't missed out any topics. Brush up on any areas of difficulty by talking them over with a friend or getting help from your teacher.
- Attend any revision classes put on by your teacher. Remember, your teacher is an expert at preparing people for examinations.

REVISED

The day before the examination

- Flick through these Revision Notes for useful reminders, for example the 'remember' tips, key terms, summaries and exam skills.
- Check the time and place of your examination.
- Make sure you have everything you need – extra pens and pencils, tissues, a watch, bottled water, sweets.
- Allow some time to relax and have an early night to ensure you are fresh and alert for the examination.

REVISED

My exams

Unit R180 paper

Date: ....

Time: ....

Location: ....

Exam breakdown

About the exam

REVISED

Unit R180 **Reducing the risk of sports injuries and dealing with common medical conditions** is the only exam-based unit on the OCR Level 1/Level 2 Cambridge National in Sport Science and it counts for 40% of your overall qualification weighting. It is therefore important to understand the content to be covered, how the exam is structured and the different types of questions you are likely to face.

Your exam paper examines five topics from the specification:
+ Different factors which influence the risk and severity of injury.
+ Warm-up and cool down routines.
+ Different types and causes of sports injuries.
+ Reducing risk, treatment and rehabilitation of sports injuries and medical conditions.
+ Causes, symptoms and treatment of medical conditions.

Your paper is 75 minutes long and is worth 70 marks, so you have one minute per mark and five minutes at the end to check through your answers.

Question types

REVISED

On your exam paper, there will be a range of different question types such as true/false, multiple choice, completion of tables and extended answer questions. These questions have three performance objectives:
+ PO1: answers here require recall knowledge and an understanding.
+ PO2: answers to these questions require you to apply knowledge and understanding.
+ PO3: answers to these questions require you to analyse and evaluate knowledge, understanding and performance.

Section A: contains 25 marks for simple recall questions so the focus is on PO1. These questions will either be multiple choice questions or lead with a simple requirement to 'state' or 'identify' something, for example, identify three different types of acute injury that can occur at the ankle.

Section B: contains 45 marks and includes short- and medium-answer questions which are focused more on PO2 with some PO1. PO2 means you need to apply your knowledge and questions may ask you to use practical examples to illustrate application of knowledge and understanding, for example, using a practical example, describe how tendonitis can occur at the ankle joint.

This section also contains the eight-mark extended question. This question needs to be answered in more depth and is assessed against a 'levels' mark scheme. These levels have statements related to the written quality of your answer. This means that the examiner needs to be able to read your answer, so keep your handwriting neat. You also have to write in a structured way with accurate spelling, punctuation and grammar and use specialist terminology where you can, to achieve the higher levels. In addition, each level includes a list of the required content you need to include to achieve that level.

Example of levels of response descriptions	
Level 3 (7–8 marks)	A thorough discussion which: + shows detailed knowledge and understanding + analyses the points made, showing logical reasoning throughout and reaching a justified conclusion (where one is required) + consistently uses appropriate terminology.
Level 2 (4–6 marks)	A response-adequate discussion: + shows sound knowledge and understanding + analyses the points made; may show some logical reasoning + uses some appropriate terminology.
Level 1 (1–3 marks)	A basic discussion: + shows limited knowledge and understanding + limited analysis of points made; may lack logic + limited or no use of appropriate terminology.
0 = nil response or no response worthy of credit.	

Command words

REVISED

When sitting your exam, read each question carefully and identify exactly what is required. You might want to highlight or underline to understand what the question is asking for. If you do this, always highlight the command word, as this will help you to plan the content of your answer.

The following command words could be used in your exam questions and there is an explanation to help you understand what each command word requires you to do.

+ **Analyse** – separate or break down information into parts and identify their characteristics or elements.
+ **Annotate** – add information, for example, to a table, diagram or graph until it is final.
+ **Calculate** – get a numerical answer showing how it has been worked out.
+ **Choose** – select an answer from options given.
+ **Circle** – select an answer from options given.
+ **Compare and contrast** – give an account of the similarities and differences between two or more items or situations.
+ **Complete** – add all the needed or appropriate parts/add information, for example, to a table, diagram or graph until it is final.
+ **Describe** – give an account including all the relevant characteristics, qualities or events/give a detailed account of …
+ **Discuss** – present, analyse and evaluate relevant points (for example, for/against an argument).
+ **Evaluate** – make a reasoned qualitative judgement considering different factors and using available knowledge/experience.
+ **Explain** – give reasons for and/or causes of. Use the words 'because' or 'therefore' in answers.
+ **Fill in** – add all the needed or appropriate parts/add information, for example, to a table, diagram or graph until it is final.
+ **Identify** – give an answer to answer the question set/select an answer from options given/recognise, name or provide factors or features.
+ **Justify** – give good reasons for offering an opinion or reaching a conclusion.
+ **Label** – add information, for example, to a table, diagram or graph until it is final/add all the necessary or appropriate parts.
+ **Outline** – give a short account, summary or description.
+ **State** – give factors or features/give short, factual answers (often linked to a specific number in the question).

- **Using practical examples** – show your full understanding of a point by using relevant practical/sporting examples linked to the requirements of the question set.

Key points to remember in the exam

REVISED

- When writing your answer produce a response that is clear and concise. Try not to waffle.
- Make sure you do not repeat information that is already given in the wording of the question.
- If a question wants you to apply your knowledge and understanding, you need to use examples.
- Look at how many parts there are to a question and make sure you answer all of them.
- Check how many marks your question is worth and match your answers to the number of marks in the question.
- Try not to miss out any questions. You could pick up a mark with an educated guess!
- You do not have to answer the questions in order. If you do not know the answer straight away do not spend time being stuck – move onto a question you can do and come back later.
- Write clearly in the spaces provided in the answer booklet.
- Avoid writing anything you want to be marked in the margins and always indicate if you run out of space that your answer continues on additional paper or at the end of the answer booklet if there is space.

Revising for your exam

REVISED

There are lots of different ways to revise for your exam and you may find that some revision methods are better than others. Here are some ideas to help you:

- **Mind maps:** read through a topic and then without your notes put the key points into a mind map. Check to see if you have covered everything and if not add the missing knowledge to the mind map. You will then have a concise version of your topic notes. A mind map for key components of a warm-up could look like that shown below:

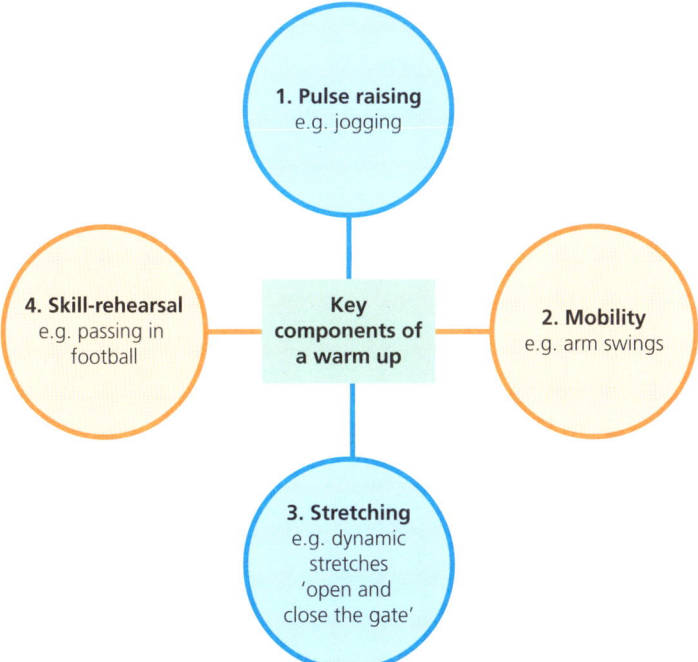

+ **Exam questions:** as well as the practice questions later in this book, you can also visit the OCR website where there are lots of past papers and mark schemes. You can use these to test your knowledge. You will also become familiar with the types of questions that could appear on your paper. Try to answer a whole paper in 75 minutes without stopping, so that you get used to the amount of time you have available. This will prepare you for exam conditions.
+ **Revision cards:** simply read a topic and rewrite your notes briefly onto small cards. Make sure you include all the main points. You may also wish to put notes on one side of the card and questions and answers on the other side.
+ **Study buddy:** revise with a friend and test one another.

Topic area 1: Different factors which influence the risk and severity of injury

1.1 Extrinsic factors

REVISED

An **extrinsic factor** that can influence the risk and severity of injury is something that is external to the body.

1.1.1 Types of sports activity

How different sporting activities can influence types of injury

Contact sports

A **contact sport** is a sport in which there is physical contact between performers.

The injuries sustained in these sports often occur as a result of impact. Full contact sports run a high risk of injury.
+ Martial arts such as judo require physical contact with opponents for a participant to score points.
+ In boxing, points are scored when making contact with an opponent.
+ Rugby requires contact in tackling.

Other sports such as netball and basketball do not involve as much contact.
+ The rules of the game try to reduce this; the umpire can award penalties or fouls when contact is made.
+ They are, however, still contact sports as contact is inevitable when contesting for a ball.
+ Injuries in these sports tend to occur more through muscle strains and sprains as there is a lot of running, jumping and twisting.
+ Injuries can also be caused by contact with equipment. For example, two players running to get to a ball and colliding with the goal post.

> **Extrinsic factors** Risk or factor that causes an injury that comes from outside the body.
>
> **Contact sport** A sport in which there is physical contact between performers.

> **Typical mistake**
>
> Do not be misled by the term 'contact'. A contact sport is not just combat sports such as boxing but can be a rugby game in which players make contact in a tackle.

Figure 1.1 Judo is a contact sport

Non-contact sports

A non-contact sport is where there is no physical contact.

+ Gymnastics and dance are non-contact sports. Injuries in these activities tend to occur through falls and landing incorrectly, such as a sprained ankle or knee.
+ Most net games, such as tennis and badminton, are non-contact sports. Injuries in these sports are more likely to be caused by twisting to change direction quickly, or overuse injuries such as tennis elbow from repeated actions (such as playing the same shots).

Non-contact sport A sport in which players are kept apart and any physical contact is penalised, for example, in netball the umpire will award a penalty pass.

Tennis elbow A condition that causes pain around the outside of the elbow caused by repeated stress on the elbow tendons.

Figure 1.2 Netball is a non-contact sport. If there is any contact, a penalty is awarded

> **Exam tip**
>
> If types of sports activities appear in an extended question, make sure you develop your points. Do not just list different types of activity, you also need to explain the differences between activities and give examples of injuries that can occur.

> **Now test yourself** TESTED
>
> Choose **five** contact and **five** non-contact sports and list the type of injuries that are common in each of these activities.

> **Check your understanding**
>
> 1 State **two** injuries that can occur in contact sports.
> 2 State **two** injuries that can occur in non-contact sports.

1.1.2 Coaching/instructing/leading

Knowledge of techniques/rules/regulations

Techniques

A coach who teaches poor or incorrect technique increases the risk of injury.

+ In rugby, good tackling technique is important. Head position during a tackle and where the shoulders make contact should be coached correctly to avoid shoulder and neck injuries.
+ In football, coaching good tackling technique can avoid injuries to the player being tackled. A correctly coached player will have much better timing and accuracy of contact than a player who has been poorly coached.
+ In high jump, the take-off foot should be planted correctly on the ground so that the take-off is straight and therefore does not place unnecessary stress on the ankle joint.
+ A poor coach may also encourage aggressive (and therefore dangerous) play such as a two-footed tackle in football.

Technique Method used to perform a skill.

Rules and regulations

Not adhering to rules and regulations can lead to injury.

+ Before a sporting activity, a coach should check that players are wearing any compulsory protective equipment and also ensure that they continue to do so throughout the activity, for example, wearing goggles in squash to protect the eyes.
+ A coach or supervisor should also check that children are playing in the correct age group, because an older child may be bigger and stronger and cause injury to a smaller child on contact.
+ A player who does not adhere to the rules and is being penalised for unnecessary contact should be substituted by a coach. They may be able to return to the activity later on.

Experience

An experienced coach/instructor/leader will have the necessary knowledge and skills to reduce the risk of injury.

+ They will have had plenty of practice planning and delivering sports activities in a safe and controlled manner and be fully qualified.
+ They will be able to identify risky activities within the sport they are coaching, such as tackling in football and rugby or landing from a vault in gymnastics, and will ensure that correct technique is used to reduce the risk of injury.
+ An experienced coach will also provide advice on the correct use of equipment, for example, using the correct grip on a tennis racket to reduce the risk of an injury such as tendonitis.

Tendonitis Inflammation of the tendons.

Figure 1.3 Coach supporting a gymnast

Communication

Good communication is essential for avoiding injuries.

+ Some sporting activities can be potentially dangerous. When coaching javelin to a group of children, for example, it is essential to communicate effectively with clear instructions when to retrieve the javelin so it is not thrown towards them.
+ Not explaining an activity correctly can also increase the risk of injury, for example, not raising a hockey stick too high where it becomes dangerous.
+ In large groups, coaches and supervisors need to be heard clearly by all performers.

Supervision

Poor supervision in a sports session increases the risk of injury.
+ Inadequate supervision could lead to poor behaviour among participants.
+ The number of participants will influence the amount of supervision needed. The greater the number of participants, the more supervision required.
+ Supervision should take place close to the activity so that it is easy to observe all participants. For example, a coach who allows players to continue to practise while they tidy up equipment is not focusing on the players, who could get injured.
+ The nature of the activity will influence the type of supervision needed. More general supervision is required in low-risk activities such as a game of badminton where a coach may just walk around to observe players. However, in higher-risk activities, such as learning to vault in gymnastics, much closer supervision is required.

Figure 1.4 Coach supervising a group of rugby players

Ethical standards/behaviour

A coach/leader/instructor needs to be aware that they are a role model for their players and that poor ethical standards or behaviour can be easily copied.
+ A coach needs to ensure fair play, for example, following the rules. If a coach encourages foul play it can lead to injury.
+ A 'win at all costs' attitude could lead to players returning to play before they have fully recovered from an injury.
+ A coach should manage emotions to demonstrate self-control. A coach with poor self-control can influence players. For example, a player may copy the behaviour of an overly aggressive and frustrated basketball coach. This player might then become reckless as they compete for a ball in the air and cause injury.

> **Exam tip**
>
> Do not forget there are five areas to consider under the coaching/instructing/leading section so, in extended questions, all five need to be mentioned to score the highest marks.

> **Now test yourself** — TESTED
>
> Compile a list of **five** behaviours that make a good coach.

> **Check your understanding**
>
> 3 Describe **three** ways in which an experienced coach can reduce the risk of injury.
> 4 Describe **three** ways in which poor supervision in a sports session can increase the risk of injury.

Check your understanding and progress at www.hoddereducation.co.uk/myrevisionnotes

1.1.3 Environment

Weather/temperature conditions
Some injuries can occur because it is too hot or too cold.
+ Hot weather means there is an increased risk of dehydration, heat exhaustion, heat stroke and sunburn. To avoid this, wherever possible, activities should take place in the shade.
+ In very cold conditions, there is an increased risk of hypothermia. Warming up also becomes harder, leading to a higher risk of muscle strains and tears.
+ Foggy weather and bright sunlight reduce visibility, and rain can make surfaces slippery, increasing the risk of injuries such as bruises, cuts and broken bones.

> **Dehydration** Occurs when the body loses more fluid than is taken in, leading to headaches, dizziness and feeling tired.
>
> **Heat exhaustion** Occurs as a result of prolonged exposure to excessive or unaccustomed heat, leading to fatigue and collapse.
>
> **Heat stroke** Occurs when the body fails to regulate temperature, leading to fever and unconsciousness.
>
> **Hypothermia** Occurs when the body temperature drops dangerously low, leading to shivering, slurred speech and tiredness.

Figure 1.5 Long-distance runners need to avoid heat exhaustion in hot and sunny conditions

> **Exam tip**
>
> Consider links with other topic areas here, for example, how hot/cold weather conditions can affect medical conditions (Topic area 5: Causes, symptoms and treatment of medical conditions).

Playing surface (natural and artificial) and surrounding area
Before a game or training session starts, the playing surface or performance area needs to be checked for safety.
+ Wet conditions make a playing surface slippery, and very cold conditions can freeze the playing surface, making the ground too hard to play on. In these conditions, a game should be cancelled.
+ The surrounding area should also be checked for injury risks, for example, corner flags should be secure.
+ In sports halls, there may be benches or nets or other equipment around the side that need to be removed.
+ Playing surfaces outside need to be checked for hazards such as glass, wet leaves and dog faeces.

Figure 1.6 Playing football in the snow can make the AstroTurf slippery

> **Exam tip**
>
> Try to make links between the playing surface and other extrinsic factors such as wearing moulded studs on a hard, dry pitch and studs on soft ground.

Human interaction

Other performers/participants

There are many other competitors in team games. This increases the risk of collisions or rule infringements, such as fouls, that can cause injury. Some participants could be too aggressive, over competitive, or may behave in a silly or reckless manner. In addition, all participants need to ensure they are wearing appropriate equipment and footwear, nails are short, hair is tied back and jewellery is removed.

Officials

Officials can play an important role in reducing the risk of injury before and during the game. They interact with coaches and players before the game regarding safety checks on the playing surface and surrounding area, and regarding clothing and footwear. During a game, officials interact with coaches, players and spectators to explain decisions and reduce frustration.

How an official communicates with players is also important. An official who speaks aggressively or shouts a lot may cause a player to become frustrated in a match and start to play dangerously. Effective and clear communication is required when an official interacts with a player, for example, to ensure that a rugby player understands instructions during a scrum.

Spectators

Good spectators can boost morale and encourage a good performance. However, sometimes the behaviour of spectators can lead to injuries. Aggressive and argumentative supporters can encourage deviant player behaviour, such as retaliation/revenge on an opponent who has fouled/injured them earlier in the game. Having spectators too close to the court/pitch can also lead to injury from collisions.

Figure 1.7 Spectators are close to the action during basketball matches

> **Now test yourself** TESTED
>
> Choose one outdoor team game and give one example each of how the weather, playing surface and other participants can influence the risk of injury.

> **Check your understanding**
>
> 5 Describe **three** ways in which the playing surface and surrounding area can increase the risk of injury.
> 6 State **two** safety checks an official should carry out before a sporting activity.

> **Exam tip**
>
> Try to make links between human interaction and other extrinsic factors, for example, the effect on a participant of an official making poor decisions.

1.1.4 Equipment

Protective equipment

Examples of protective equipment include shin pads in football, gumshields in boxing and rugby, helmets in cycling and goggles in skiing.

+ Shin and ankle pads are worn in football as these are the two areas that are most likely to be damaged by impact in a tackle.
+ Gumshields are worn in boxing as contact is often to the face, and teeth need protecting.
+ Helmets are worn in cycling and skiing as protection from head injuries, as these performers travel at high speed.
+ Goggles protect the eyes. A skier goes very fast and will not be able to react quickly enough to protect their eyes if they come into contact with anything.

Protective equipment can also be found on buildings and objects involved in sport, such as around posts. In netball and rugby, the goal posts and sticks are padded in case of collision.

Performance equipment

This includes hockey sticks, cricket balls and a harness in climbing.

+ Equipment should be checked to make sure it is safe and not damaged.
+ A ball should be checked to see how hard or soft it is and whether there are any rough edges. This is particularly important in football, as players head the ball.
+ Some balls, such as cricket and hockey balls, are very hard, and with this comes the risk of injury.
+ A harness in climbing must always be checked before a climb begins, as it can potentially save a life.

Figure 1.8 A skier wears a helmet for protection

Clothing

Clothing should be suitable for the weather and slightly loose, but not so loose that it could catch on something.

+ When the weather is hot, loose clothing and breathable fabrics are important to try to keep the body cool and prevent overheating.
+ In cold conditions, wearing a T-shirt and shorts outside would not keep the muscles warm and could lead to injury. Waterproof clothing is also important in sports such as skiing to keep warm.

Some sports have specific clothing such as a leotard in gymnastics, which is tight-fitting, almost like a second skin. This is worn for safety reasons because loose clothing can catch on the equipment. A leotard also ensures that the judges can see the gymnast's movements clearly. A triathlete wears a tri-suit throughout the whole race. It is made of quick-drying fabric, which is essential after the swim, and has a small pad in the shorts for protection during cycling.

Figure 1.9 Triathletes wear the same tri-suit for the swim, cycle and run

Footwear

Wearing suitable footwear for the playing surface and weather conditions can help to avoid injury.

+ On AstroTurf, players need to wear AstroTurf trainers or moulded studs to prevent slipping.
+ On hard, dry ground, moulded studs should be worn as most moulded boots have a large number of studs that give better support and reduce the risk of blisters.
+ In wet conditions and boggy pitches, football players should wear soft-ground studs to gain a better grip.
+ For indoor sports such as basketball and netball, trainers need to be tied up correctly and have a good sole that has not worn out to prevent sprains and strains.

Figure 1.10 Hockey shoes have a suitable sole for AstroTurf pitches to prevent slipping

Now test yourself TESTED

Identify the protective equipment worn by a cricketer, squash player and cyclist.

Exam tip

Make sure you can identify and explain with examples how equipment can influence the risk of injury. For example, no padding around a netball post can lead to a head injury if a player makes contact with the metal post with their head.

Check your understanding

7 Explain, giving **two** examples, how equipment can influence the risk of injury in sport.
8 Explain, giving **two** examples, how clothing and footwear can lead to injury in sport.

Check your understanding and progress at www.hoddereducation.co.uk/myrevisionnotes

1.2 Intrinsic factors

REVISED

An intrinsic factor, which influences the risk of injury, is a factor that comes from within your body.

> **Intrinsic factors** A risk or factor that causes an injury that comes from inside the body.
>
> **Fatigue** A feeling of overwhelming tiredness.

> **Exam tip**
>
> Make sure you can link the extrinsic factors with the intrinsic factors, for example, human interaction and psychological factors or link this topic area with other topics, for example, coaching (Topic area 1) with a warm-up or cool down routine (Topic area 2).

1.2.1 Individual variables

One player may be different from another in terms of individual variables such as gender, age, weight and experience. Each of these differences can mean that one participant is more likely to suffer a sports injury than the next. You need to have knowledge of how the following individual variables can influence the risk and severity of injury.

Gender

On average, males tend to be stronger than females and females tend to be more flexible than males. Therefore, an (average) female trying to lift the same amount of weight as an (average) male, and likewise, an (average) male trying to produce the same range of movement as an (average) female, may have a higher risk of injury. In addition, contact sports such as rugby tend to be played professionally in either all-male or all-female teams, rather than mixed, to reduce the risk of injury.

Age

The older the player, the more prone to injury they are. This is because older people are generally less flexible and have less strength than younger adults. Equally, children are smaller than adults, able to lift less weight and may require specialist equipment to avoid injury, for example, lighter bats or smaller shin pads.

Experience

An experienced player can reduce the risk of injury through better knowledge of sports technique and correct use of equipment. They will make sure they have rest days to avoid overtraining and will know the importance of a good diet and plenty of sleep. In addition, they will be aware of injury prevention strategies such as conditioning to strengthen muscles.

Weight

A performer who is either overweight or underweight can increase the risk of injury.
+ Being overweight has many health implications, such as an increased risk of heart disease, but in sport it can also lead to stress fractures in the lower legs.
+ Being underweight can lead to fatigue and this can result in a lack of concentration while playing sport, which in turn can lead to injury through collisions, poor balance or a deterioration in technique.

Fitness levels

A poor level of cardiovascular fitness can mean a performer will fatigue more easily.
+ Someone who is tired is more likely to make errors in their technique and this can influence the risk of injury.
+ Poor strength also results in weaker muscles that are quick to fatigue, so posture can be affected.
+ Limited flexibility may also cause overstretching of a muscle or cause a performer to use poor technique, which could then lead to an injury.

Technique/ability

Incorrect technique can increase the risk of injury. For example, poor technique in weightlifting can result in back injuries, and poor throwing technique can lead to shoulder and elbow injuries.

Nutrition/hydration

Having the correct, balanced diet is very important in reducing injuries.
+ A poor diet that does not include enough calories or carbohydrates may cause a performer to be too tired and to lack sufficient energy to complete a training session or sporting event, which could lead to fainting or dizziness.
+ A poor diet can also affect concentration and focus, increasing the likelihood of a performer becoming distracted. When this occurs, technique deteriorates, which could lead to injury, for example, a badly timed jump in basketball that could lead to a collision.
+ Too much fat in a diet will lead to weight gain, which puts more pressure on joints, leading to injury such as stress fractures.
+ A lack of certain minerals or vitamins can lead to weak bones and muscles, which could lead to more injuries such as muscle tears.
+ Finally, a lack of water leads to dehydration, resulting in dizziness, fatigue and a deterioration in performance.

> **Cardiovascular fitness** The ability of the body to take in and use oxygen while exercising.
>
> **Carbohydrates** Nutrients that should form the main source of energy.
>
> **Stress fractures** Tiny cracks in a bone caused by repetitive force, often from overuse.
>
> **Minerals and vitamins** Substances needed for many essential functions of the body.

Figure 1.11 Nutrition is important in preventing injuries

Medical conditions

There are lots of medical conditions that can increase the risk of injury. These are discussed in more detail in Topic area 5. Some examples include asthma, diabetes and hyperthermia.
+ Individuals who have severe asthma are unlikely to be involved in vigorous sporting activities because asthma can lead to a severe shortage of breath.

> **Asthma** A condition in which the airways narrow and swell, which can make breathing difficult.
>
> **Diabetes** A condition in which blood sugar levels are not regulated by the body effectively.
>
> **Hyperthermia** Occurs when an athlete's body temperature rises and remains above the normal temperature of 37 °C (98.6 °F).

- A person with diabetes needs to consider what they eat before and during exercise, as sport can cause changes in blood sugar. Failure to manage blood sugar can lead to serious medical conditions such as hypoglycaemia or hyperglycaemia.
- Exercising also causes body temperature to rise and if this cannot be controlled it could lead to hyperthermia.

Sleep
Lots of exercise means you will need long and good-quality sleep.
- Some of the rebuilding of the damage done to muscle cells caused by strenuous exercise is done during sleep. Deep sleep is important for muscle recovery. Therefore, a lack of deep sleep prevents muscle recovery, making muscles more susceptible to injury.
- Poor sleep can also lead to fatigue and reduced concentration levels; and it can make an individual irritable and aggressive. These can all influence injury through poor judgement and decision-making, leading to dangerous play such as an overly aggressive or mistimed interception in netball.

Previous/recurring injuries
Having a previous injury can often increase the chance of the same injury recurring. With an ankle sprain, for example, the ligaments are damaged and the performer has to rest to enable it to recover. This leads to a loss of fitness, and muscles and tendons around the joint become weaker. If rehabilitation is not done correctly to strengthen the soft tissue around the ankle, there is a high risk of the same injury recurring.

> **Hyperglycaemia** Occurs when blood sugars are too high.
>
> **Hypoglycaemia** Occurs when blood sugars are too low.
>
> **Ligaments** Fibrous tissue that connects bone to bone and strengthens joints.
>
> **Motivation** A person's drive to succeed.

> **Typical mistake**
>
> Do not muddle the terms hyperthermia and hypothermia – they look very similar but have different meanings.

> **Now test yourself** TESTED
>
> Make a list of all the individual variables and give an example of how each one can increase the risk of injury.

> **Exam tip**
>
> Make sure you can apply your knowledge of these individual variables to that of reducing the risk of injury, rather than just describing each variable. For example, do not just explain why we need sleep, instead discuss how a lack of sleep can lead to injury.

> **Check your understanding**
>
> 9 State **three** ways in which the age and weight of a performer can increase the risk of injury.
> 10 State **two** reasons why the fitness level of a performer is an important factor in reducing injury.

1.2.2 Psychological factors
A performer's frame of mind can either result in more injuries or reduce the chance of them. Many elite sports teams employ a sports psychologist to help reduce the number of injuries caused by a lack of player-focus before a match. Being in the right frame of mind can help prevent injuries occurring, but being in the wrong frame of mind increases the risk of injury. (See Topic area 2.2.2 for more on the psychological benefits of doing a warm-up). The following psychological factors can influence the risk of injury.

Motivation
Motivation is a person's desire to succeed.
- An increase in motivation increases drive and could lead to recklessness in contesting for a ball, resulting in injury.
- A lack of motivation decreases drive and could cause injury because a player may not commit themselves to an activity. For example, pulling out of a rebound in basketball and colliding with another player.

Arousal

Arousal is the level of body and mind stimulation that gets us ready to perform, and levels of arousal are important in influencing the risk of injury.

+ Over-arousal may result in the performer being too reckless or overly aggressive. In a football tackle, displaying these emotions could lead to an injury.
+ Underarousal results in a lack of confidence. For example, not being able to commit to a tackle can also lead to injury.
+ To avoid injury, a performer, therefore, needs to be able to control their arousal levels so that they make safe decisions and keep their focus.

Anxiety/stress

Anxiety negatively affects performance because a performer becomes too nervous or worried. These feelings could lead to a lack of effort, due to a fear of failing. It can reduce concentration and focus, and increase the risk of injury. For example, poor timing to intercept a pass in netball and making contact with an opponent.

Stress is the response of an individual to a threat. It can occur in sport during games when a player feels frustrated or angry or just before a competition when feeling nervous.

Confidence

Being overconfident can increase the risk of injury because it may lead to a performer not putting in the required effort. For example, they may feel they are much better than those on the opposing team so do not prepare properly for their match. On the other hand, lack of confidence could lead to a lack of belief in ability. An example could be not fully committing to collecting a rebound ball if the performer believes their opponent is much better than them, which could result in unnecessary contact.

Aggression

Aggression is forceful action caused by feelings of hostility or anger, and can cause harm to others so needs to be controlled to avoid injury. Too much aggression can lead to a lack of control and negatively affects technique. An example is a reckless tackle in hockey or rugby.

Direct

Direct aggression involves physical contact with others, for example, punching or kicking another player.

> **Arousal** The level of body and mind stimulation that gets us ready to perform.
>
> **Anxiety** When a performer experiences worry, nervousness and apprehension.
>
> **Stress** A person's reaction to feeling threatened or under pressure.
>
> **Aggression** Forceful action caused by feelings of hostility or anger, which can cause harm to others.
>
> **Direct aggression** Involves physical contact with others.

Figure 1.12 Aggression needs to be controlled to avoid injury

Check your understanding and progress at www.hoddereducation.co.uk/myrevisionnotes

Channelled

Channelled aggression is where feelings of aggression are diverted into more positive actions and become controlled. They are not intended to harm but an injury could still occur, for example, a hard and fair tackle in rugby or a throw in judo.

> **Channelled aggression** When feelings of aggression are diverted into positive, productive actions.
>
> **Retaliation** The act of harming someone because they have harmed you.

> **Now test yourself** TESTED
>
> Identify **three** psychological factors and give an example of how each factor can increase the risk of injury.

> **Check your understanding**
>
> 11 Explain, giving **two** reasons, how anxiety can increase the risk of injury.
> 12 Explain the difference between direct and channelled aggression.

1.2.3 Reasons for aggression

The reasons for aggression are difficult to identify but a number of possible causes have been suggested.

Level of performance

Performers may become frustrated and aggressive for a number of reasons such as:
+ losing a game that they felt they should be winning due to poor personal performance
+ poor performance of another teammate or their team
+ their opponent is too good.

Retaliation

A player who is fouled in a game of football may experience frustration, which can lead to retaliation resulting in a push or a punch to the player who fouled them. Retaliation is a form of revenge and is a common cause of aggression in many contact sports.

Pressures to win (performer/coach/spectators)

Many performers are put under a lot of pressure to win from teammates, spectators and coaches and this can lead to over arousal and aggression. They may be expected to perform well because of the need for success, the status of the competition or financial incentives. This pressure to win can lead to strong emotions, resulting in poor technique or, for example, a reckless attempt to gain possession of the ball in netball leading to dangerous contact.

Decisions of officials

A player could become aggressive if they disagree with the decisions of a referee or feel that the official's decisions are unfair. For example, not agreeing with the awarding of a penalty in football or a free throw in basketball could result in frustration and aggression during the match, leading to excessive contact when trying to win possession of the ball.

Performance-enhancing drugs

Performance-enhancing drugs such as steroids can cause several negative side effects including aggression, rage or violence. This can lead to dangerous play, such as a deliberate stick-foul in hockey.

> **Exam tip**
>
> Links can be made between the types of injury (Topic area 3: Different types and causes of sports injuries) caused by aggression.

> **Now test yourself**
>
> Make a list of the possible reasons for aggression and give an example for each reason of an injury that could occur.
> TESTED

> **Check your understanding**
>
> 13 Explain, giving **two** reasons, how the decision of a referee could lead to injury.

1.2.4 Mental strategies

The following mental strategies can reduce the risk of injury, as they can help reduce anxiety and stress and improve focus and concentration.

Mental rehearsal

Mental rehearsal involves practising the movements of a skill or technique in your head so that you are ready to perform it in a match. For example, a shooter in netball could rehearse the movements involved in their shooting action. It is best done in a calm situation prior to the event.

Imagery

Imagery is where a performer recreates a successful image of an action from a past performance in which a skill was performed correctly and the performer can recall the feel of the actual movements. For example, a football player can picture themselves taking a successful penalty and a tennis player can picture a successful serve.

> **Mental rehearsal** When a performer goes over the movements of a task in the mind before the action takes place.
>
> **Imagery** Enables a performer to picture a successful performance in their head to reduce stress.
>
> **Selective attention** Filtering out irrelevant information.

Figure 1.13 These rowers are using mental rehearsal to improve performance

Selective attention

Selective attention helps to improve focus and is where a performer identifies the information they need and disregards the information they do not need. In a doubles badminton match, for example, the player would focus on their opponents, the flight of the shuttlecock and the position of their doubles partner and ignore what is outside the court such as spectators. Poor ability to use selective attention on court could result in injury, for example, if the badminton player failed to notice the position of their doubles partner, a collision could occur.

> **Exam tip**
>
> Links can be made between mental strategies and warm-up routines in Topic area 2. Part of a warm-up may include mental rehearsal.

Now test yourself — TESTED

Explain mental rehearsal, imagery and selective attention.

Check your understanding

14 Explain the difference between mental rehearsal and imagery.

Check your understanding and progress at www.hoddereducation.co.uk/myrevisionnotes

Exam checklist

In 1.1, you learned about the **extrinsic factors** that can affect the risk and severity of injury. These factors include:

+ How contact and non-contact sporting activities can influence types of injury.
+ How coaches, instructors and leaders can influence the risk and severity of injury through knowledge of techniques/rules/regulations, their experience, communication, supervision and ethical standards/behaviour.
+ The effect the environment can have on the risk of injury with the focus on the weather/temperature conditions, the type of playing surface and surrounding area as well the human interaction between performers, officials and spectators.
+ The importance of protective equipment, performance equipment, clothing and footwear in reducing the risk and severity of injury.

In 1.2, you learned about the **intrinsic factors** and how they can affect the risk and severity of injury. These factors include:

+ Individual variables such as gender, age, experience, weight, fitness levels, technique/ability, nutrition/hydration, medical conditions, sleep and previous/recurring injuries.
+ The psychological factors of motivation, arousal, anxiety/stress, confidence and direct and channelled aggression.
+ How factors such as the level of performance, retaliation, pressures to win, decisions of officials and performance-enhancing drugs affect aggression.
+ How mental strategies such as mental rehearsal, imagery and selective attention help motivation, arousal, anxiety, stress and aggression.

Exam-style questions

1 Identify **two** types of sporting activity and give examples how each type of activity can influence the risk of injury. [3]

2 Using an example, state **three** ways that a coach can reduce the risk of injury to sports performers. [3]

3 State **three** ways that the environment can influence the risk of injury for a sports performer. [3]

4 State **four** intrinsic factors that can influence injury. [4]

5 Identify which **one** of the following is an individual variable: [2]

Choose the correct answer.
  a Coaching.
  b Equipment.
  c Environment.
  d Experience.

6 In a game of cricket, name **one** piece of performance equipment and one piece of protective equipment. [2]

7 State **three** extrinsic factors that can influence injury. [3]

8 Identify **two** results of aggression in a game of rugby. [2]

9 Describe **two** ways that poor sleep can affect the risk of an injury. [2]

10 Using a practical example, describe **two** ways that human interaction can cause injury in contact sports. [2]

11 Describe **two** ways that an increase in motivation and arousal might lead to a player suffering an injury. [2]

12 Explain the intrinsic factors that a referee needs to be aware of both before and during a match in a contact sport in order to reduce the risk of injury to the players. [8]

Topic area 2: Warm-up and cool down routines

2.1 Key components of a warm-up

REVISED

Warm-ups are simple exercise routines that prepare the body for physical activity. They can have a positive effect on the body and behaviour of a performer, improving the quality of the performance and lowering the risk of injury.

2.1.1 Key components of a warm-up

Warm-ups can vary depending on the person and the activity. There are four key components of a warm-up:

+ Pulse raising.
+ Mobility.
+ Dynamic stretching.
+ Skill-rehearsal phase.

You need to understand the order of each part of a warm-up and what activities you are required to do so that you are ready to participate in your activity and avoid injury.

Pulse raising

The first part of a warm-up should be a pulse raiser. This involves doing activities such as running for a games player, cycling for a cyclist or swimming a few lengths for a swimmer, which will slowly increase the heart rate and raise muscle temperature. Increasing heart rate will mean more oxygenated blood will get to the working muscles.

> **Warm-up** Exercises to prepare the body for exercise so that the chances of injury or ill effects are reduced.
>
> **Pulse raising** An activity that increases heart rate.
>
> **Mobility** Swinging exercises to increase the range of motion.
>
> **Dynamic stretches** Moving stretches that increase the range of motion of a joint.
>
> **Skill rehearsal** Practising common movements and skills.
>
> **Oxygenated** Arterial blood (in arteries) that carries oxygen.

Figure 2.1 Pulse-raising activity

Mobility

Next up is mobility. This involves taking a joint through its full range of motion, for example, by doing exercises such as arm swings for a swimmer or golfer and leg swings for a long jumper.

Dynamic stretching

Stretching involves lengthening a muscle to increase the range of motion at a joint. Dynamic stretches involves movement as you stretch, and it is important to link this to the same movement patterns that you are going to do in your activity, for example, performing a forward lunge dynamic stretch, which you would do in a game of netball to try to catch a low ball.

Figure 2.2 Dynamic stretching activity

Skill-rehearsal phase

The final stage of a warm-up is the skill-rehearsal stage. This is where common movement patterns and skills are rehearsed, for example, shooting drills in basketball and passing drills in football. This will prepare the participant for the necessary technique and performance of skills that will be developed during a session. Skill rehearsal can also help improve reaction/response time and confidence.

> **Exam tip**
>
> It is easy to mix up stretching and mobility. Remember that stretching involves lengthening a muscle while mobility involves taking a joint thorough its full range of movement.

Figure 2.3 Skill-rehearsal phase for wheelchair basketball

> **Now test yourself** TESTED
>
> Using all four components of a warm-up, give examples of what you would do for your sporting activity.

> **Typical mistake**
>
> If asked to identify a particular warm-up component, do not make the mistake of giving an example rather than naming the component, so answer with 'pulse raiser' and not 'jogging'. If an activity example is required, the question will ask for one.

2.2 Physiological and psychological benefits of a warm-up

REVISED

A warm-up is a simple exercise routine that prepares the body for physical activity. It can have a positive effect on the body, for example, increasing heart rate so that more oxygenated blood travels to the muscles. It can also mentally prepare the performer and lower the risk of injury.

2.2.1 Physiological benefits

A warm-up helps to prepare the body physically so that it is ready for the activity that follows.

Cardiorespiratory benefits:
+ **Increase in heart rate:** this will increase blood flow and oxygen to the working muscles, and will help to delay fatigue.

Musculoskeletal benefits:
+ **Increase in muscle temperature:** this will increase the range of movement in muscles and joints which can help to avoid injury. A football player, for example, will be able to stretch further into a tackle without straining a muscle, and a badminton player will be able to reach further to play a shot.
+ **Increase in flexibility of muscles and joints:** this increases the range of movement possible through the joints.
+ **Increase in the pliability of** tendons **and** ligaments: this simply means making them more flexible and supple, which reduces the possibility of injury.
+ **Increase in blood flow and oxygen to the muscles:** more oxygen means the muscles will be slower to fatigue.
+ **Increase in the speed of muscle contraction:** this means more force can be produced, for example, in a jump ball in basketball the player will be ready to exert as much force into their jump as possible to gain as much height as they can to win the tip without the fear of injury. It will also improve reaction time so that a netball player will be able to dodge to quickly change direction to get free of their marker more successfully.

> **Cardiorespiratory system** Consists of the heart and blood vessels which work together with the lungs in the respiratory system. Together they transport oxygen to the muscles and organs of the body.
>
> **Musculoskeletal system** Includes bones, cartilage, ligaments, tendons and connective tissues.
>
> **Tendons** Soft tissue that joins muscles to bones.
>
> **Ligaments** Soft tissue that joins bone to bone.

2.2.2 Psychological benefits

During the warm-up routine, the performer will think about the activity they are about to take part in.
+ **Heighten or control arousal levels:** this prepares the performer for the activity as it allows them to 'get in the zone' or settle nerves, which in turn increases their confidence and motivation. Being over aroused can lead to rash decisions and injuries. For example, in rugby, over arousal could result in the player being too aggressive in a tackle and giving away a penalty or being sin-binned.
+ **Improve concentration and focus:** thinking about the activity will help to improve the performer's focus and concentration. Improved concentration results in quicker reaction times and faster decision-making. With greater concentration and focus, injury can also be avoided. For example, a tactical game of tennis requires lots of concentration so that the player can respond to a shot their opponent makes.
+ **Increase motivation:** thinking about the activity will increase motivation to try harder and perform better, for example, running back quickly in defence in basketball when the opposition win the ball. A lack of motivation can result in a half-hearted attempt to intercept the ball that could lead to injury.
+ **Increase confidence:** rehearsing the skills required by the activity can be done both physically and mentally (see Topic area 1.2.4 on Mental strategies). Skill rehearsal will improve technique, confidence, reaction time and overall performance.

Check your understanding and progress at www.hoddereducation.co.uk/myrevisionnotes

- **Mental rehearsal:** this involves visualising the activity and focusing on what the performer intends to do before performing it. For example, executing a successful first serve in tennis or a vault in gymnastics.

Figure 2.4 Warm-up routines prepare you for exercise

> **Now test yourself** — TESTED
>
> Compile a list of the key components of a warm-up and link the physiological benefits to these components.

> **Exam tip**
>
> Do not forget that there are psychological as well as physiological benefits of warming up so a performer can improve concentration, focus and motivation as well as control arousal levels.

> **Check your understanding**
>
> 1. State **one** example of an activity for each of the following components of a warm-up:
>   + Pulse raising.
>   + Skill rehearsal.
> 2. Explain why each of the following components of a warm-up have physiological benefits:
>   + Pulse raising.
>   + Mobility.
>   + Dynamic stretching.
>   + Skill rehearsal.
> 3. State **two** ways that the psychological benefits of a warm-up can help avoid injury.
> 4. Explain, giving **two** reasons, how the physical benefits of a warm-up can help prevent injury.

> **Typical mistake**
>
> Do not make the mistake of just learning the benefits of a warm-up. Make sure you are also aware of the possible negative effects of not performing a warm-up.

2.3 Key components of a cool down

REVISED

Sports performers should follow up a period of physical activity with **cool down** exercises so the body can return to its resting state. A cool down has two key components:
+ Pulse lowering.
+ Stretching.

> **Cool down** Easy exercises that are performed after more intense activities in order for the body to gradually move to a resting condition.

2.3.1 Pulse lowering

Pulse-lowering activities involve performing exercises that gradually lower the heart rate and breathing rate, and reduce temperature. Examples are light running or walking. These should be performed for approximately five minutes. Performers might choose to cycle or swim if these activities are more suitable.

2.3.2 Stretching

Stretching in a cool down returns the muscles used in the session back to their normal length.

Figure 2.5 Stretching to cool down

Maintenance stretches

Maintenance stretches take the muscles back to their pre-workout length. For example, after a long run, it is important to stretch leg muscles such as the hamstrings and gastrocnemius to stop them tightening up. These stretches are for muscles that already have good flexibility and range of movement and are not meant to have a big impact on flexibility. Therefore they are held for a shorter period of time (up to 30 seconds). Examples include a quadriceps stretch and side stretch.

Static stretches

Static stretching is performed in the cool down because it helps to slow the heart rate. It involves a performer moving a muscle to the end of its range of motion and holding this stretching position for a period of time, up to about 45 seconds. This stretch is then repeated two or three times. An example is bending over and touching your toes. This will help the performer remove lactic acid and prevents muscle stiffness.

Proprioceptive neuromuscular facilitation (PNF)

PNF stretching is a very effective stretching technique for increasing range of motion. It involves muscle contraction and relaxation and relies on 'switching off' protective reflexes to enable deeper stretches and greater flexibility to be achieved. A partner will gently stretch the muscle and the performer will resist the stretch by contracting the opposing muscle without moving (an isometric contraction) for about six seconds. The performer then stops applying the resistance and the partner stretches the original muscle again, which results in the muscle stretching further and deeper.

> **Maintenance stretching** For muscles that are already flexible, aiming to maintain the range of movement.
>
> **Hamstrings** A group of muscles located in the back of the thigh.
>
> **Gastrocnemius** The main calf muscle.
>
> **Static stretching** Involves holding a stretch for 30 seconds to improve flexibility.
>
> **Proprioceptive neuromuscular facilitation (PNF)** A progressive stretch involving muscle contraction and relaxation.
>
> **Isometric contraction** Where a muscle is contracting but there is no movement.

Check your understanding and progress at www.hoddereducation.co.uk/myrevisionnotes

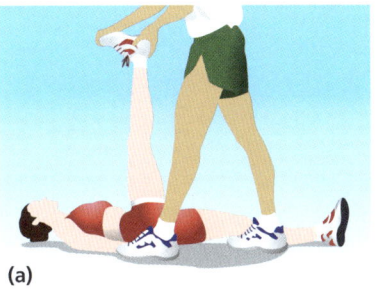 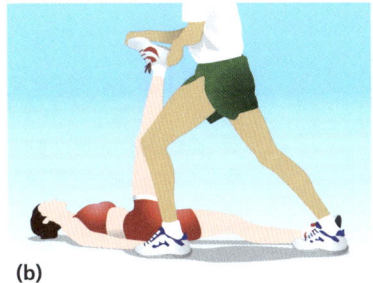 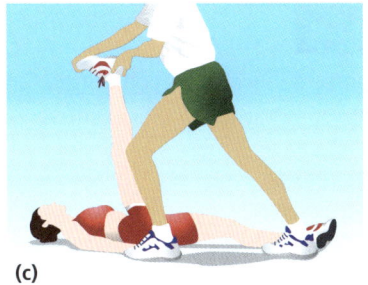

(a)   (b)   (c)

Figure 2.6 PNF stretching: (a) muscle held in stretch position; (b) isometric contraction of muscle held for six seconds; (c) second, deeper stretch

> **Now test yourself**   TESTED
>
> Link the key components of a cool down with the physical benefits of performing a cool down.

> **Exam tip**
>
> Make sure you can give examples of pulse-lowering activities and maintenance and static stretches.

2.4 Physiological benefits of a cool down

REVISED

A period of activity should be followed by additional exercises because of the physiological benefits of a cool down.

2.4.1 Physiological benefits

Performing a cool down helps the body return to its resting state. It has benefits for both the cardiorespiratory and musculoskeletal systems.

Cardiorespiratory benefits:
+ Gradually lowers heart rate.
+ Gradually lowers body temperature.
+ Gradually reduces breathing rate to pre-exercise levels.
+ Circulates blood and oxygen because stopping exercise suddenly can result in a rapid drop in heart rate and blood pressure causing light-headedness.

Musculoskeletal benefits:
+ Removes waste products such as lactic acid. Lactic acid is a by-product of working at high intensity. It increases blood acidity, which causes the muscles to fatigue.
+ Reduces the risk of delayed onset of muscle soreness (DOMS).
+ Gradually lowers muscle temperature.
+ Helps prevent blood pooling. This occurs when muscles stop contracting if light exercise does not take place and as a result it is harder to pump blood back up to the heart. This is because contracting muscles act like a pump and squeeze the veins that transport the deoxygenated blood back towards the heart. Consequently, the blood then starts to collect in legs, ankles and/or feet.

> **Lactic acid** Waste product of anaerobic exercise; causes fatigue.
>
> **Delayed onset of muscle soreness (DOMS)** A muscle pain that occurs 24–48 hours after a strenuous exercise session.

> **Exam tip**
>
> Questions might often ask you to explain how a cool down can help to avoid injury. Make sure you do not just describe a cool down – you also need to link to how a cool down prevents injury.

> **Typical mistake**
>
> Be careful how you word your answer. Saying a cool down lowers the heart rate and temperature is not specific enough – you need to explain that a cool down gradually lowers heart rate and temperature.

> **Now test yourself**   TESTED
>
> State the **two** key components of a cool down together with the physical benefits for the cardiorespiratory and musculoskeletal systems.

> **Check your understanding**
>
> 5   Identify **three** types of stretching that can be used in a cool down.
> 6   State **three** ways that light running in a cool down can help the cardiorespiratory system.
> 7   State **three** ways that stretching in a cool down can benefit the musculoskeletal system.

Topic area 2: Warm-up and cool down routines

Exam checklist

In 2.1, you learned about the key components of a warm-up. The key components of a warm-up are:
+ pulse raising
+ mobility exercises
+ dynamic stretching
+ skill-rehearsal phase.

In 2.2, you learned about the physiological and psychological benefits of performing a warm-up.
+ The physiological benefits of performing a warm-up include an increase in all of the following: muscle temperature, heart rate, flexibility of muscles and joints, pliability of ligaments and tendons, blood flow and oxygen to muscles, and speed of muscle contraction.
+ The psychological benefits of performing a warm-up allow a performer to control arousal levels, improve concentration and focus, increase motivation and confidence and provide a time for mental rehearsal to take place.

In 2.3, you learned about the key components of a cool down. The key components of a cool down are:
+ pulse-lowering exercises
+ maintenance stretches
+ static stretches
+ proprioceptive neuromuscular facilitation (PNF) stretches.

In 2.4, you learned about the physiological benefits of a cool down:
+ the gradual reduction of heart rate, temperature and breathing rate
+ prevention of blood pooling
+ removal of waste products such as lactic acid
+ reduction in the risk of delayed onset of muscle soreness (DOMS).

Exam-style questions

1. At the start of a football session, the coach needs to make sure the players complete a warm-up. Two components of a warm-up are mobility and dynamic stretching. Identify the other **two** components. [2]

2. State **one** practical example for each of the following warm-up components:
   + mobility [1]
   + dynamic stretching. [1]

3. Describe **three** psychological benefits of a warm-up. [3]

4. Describe **three** physiological benefits of a warm-up. [3]

5. Complete the table to:
   + identify a practical example for each cool down component
   + explain the main purpose of each practical example. [4]

Cool down component	Practical example	Explanation
Pulse lowering		
Maintenance stretching		

6. State **three** physiological benefits of a cool down. [3]

Topic area 3: Different types and causes of sports injuries

3.1 Acute injuries

REVISED

You need to be able to compare and contrast the causes, symptoms and treatment for each type of acute injury.

3.1.1 Overview of acute injuries
An acute injury occurs quickly and is caused by impact or a collision.

Sudden trauma
The impacts and collisions that cause acute injuries are known as sudden trauma.

Immediate impact and pain
Pain is felt straightaway and is often severe. Swelling usually occurs with a loss of function, for example, it is difficult to walk on a sprained ankle or with a broken leg bone.

> **Acute injury** Caused by sudden trauma where pain is felt immediately.
>
> **Sudden trauma** An impact that happens very quickly and causes an acute injury.
>
> **Soft tissue injuries** Injuries to muscles, tendons, ligaments and skin.
>
> **Hard tissue injuries** Injuries to the skeletal system such as fractures or dislocations.

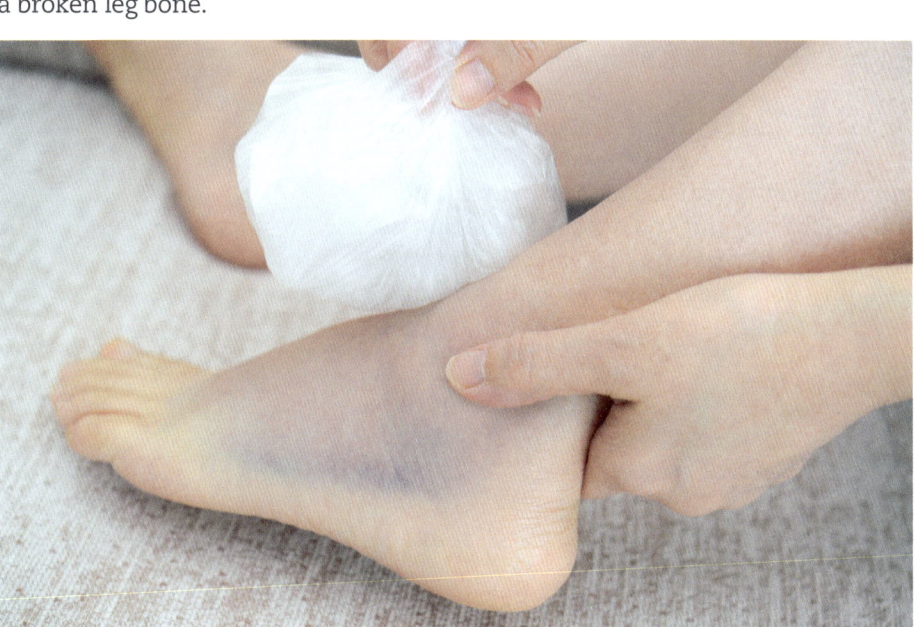

Figure 3.1 An ankle sprain

3.1.2 Soft tissue and hard tissue injuries
Acute injuries can be either soft tissue injuries or hard tissue injuries. They often occur during a collision, for example, when two players make contact in the air as they try to compete for a ball and then land awkwardly, or when a player slips in mud and sprains their ankle.

Soft tissue injuries
Soft tissue injuries happen when trauma occurs to muscles, ligaments, tendons and skin.

Hard tissue injuries

Hard tissue injuries are injuries to the skeletal system, including fractures, dislocations and teeth. A fracture can occur in a bad landing after jumping to catch a ball.

3.1.3 Strains

Strains are soft tissue injuries and can be either acute or chronic.

Torn muscle or tendon

Strains are often referred to as a 'pulled' or 'torn' muscle and a 'torn' tendon.
- **Cause:** strains occur when muscle fibres and tendons are stretched too far and tear. They occur regularly in team games where:
  - Physical contact occurs with others, for example, a tackle in football causing ankle tendon damage.
  - Landing incorrectly, for example, a poor landing after a vault in gymnastics or from an attempted interception in basketball.
  - Twisting, for example, a netball player turning and twisting as they land to face the direction of their next pass, resulting in a muscle strain.
  - Falling, for example, tripping over another player's foot causing a strain.
  - Elite athletes are also prone to strains when the intensity of their training is high and the overuse of specific muscle groups and tendons occurs regularly.
- **Symptoms:** pain, inflammation and bruising together with a lack of mobility.
- **Treatment:** see Topic area 4 (Reducing risk, treatment and rehabilitation of sports injuries and medical conditions). Initial treatment for sprain injuries includes protection, rest, ice, compression and elevation (PRICE) because these injuries will be painful and swollen and PRICE eases pain and swelling.
- **Reducing risk:** see Topic area 1 (Reducing the risk of sports injuries and dealing with common medical conditions) and Topic area 4 (Reducing risk, treatment and rehabilitation of sports injuries and medical conditions). This can be achieved through both safety checks of the playing area and the participants themselves. A coach will also need to look at the age, fitness level and experience of a group as well as any medical conditions that a participant may have.

3.1.4 Sprains

Sprains are soft tissue injuries and can be either acute or chronic.

Torn ligaments

Sprains affect ligaments, which are strong bands of tissue around joints that join bone to bone.
- **Cause:** playing sport involves lots of twisting and turning, and excessive force is often applied to a joint, so a sprain can easily occur when the ligament is stretched too far and tears. A very common injury in many sports is rolling your ankle over, resulting in a sprain.
- **Symptoms:** pain, inflammation and bruising together with a lack of mobility.
- **Treatment:** initial treatment for sprain injuries includes PRICE because these injuries will be painful and swollen and PRICE eases pain and swelling. More serious injuries, such as a complete detachment of a muscle or ligament, will require hospital treatment, such as an X-ray and possible surgery. See Topic area 4.2.
- **Reducing risk:** see Topic area 1 (Reducing the risk of sports injuries and dealing with common medical conditions) and Topic area 4 (Reducing risk, treatment and rehabilitation of sports injuries and medical conditions).

Fractures The medical term for broken bones.

Strains Injuries to muscles.

Tendon Joins muscle to bone.

PRICE An acronym for a treatment method in which the letters mean protection, rest, ice, compression and elevation.

Sprains Injuries to ligaments.

Ligaments Fibrous tissues that join bone to bone.

Check your understanding and progress at www.hoddereducation.co.uk/myrevisionnotes

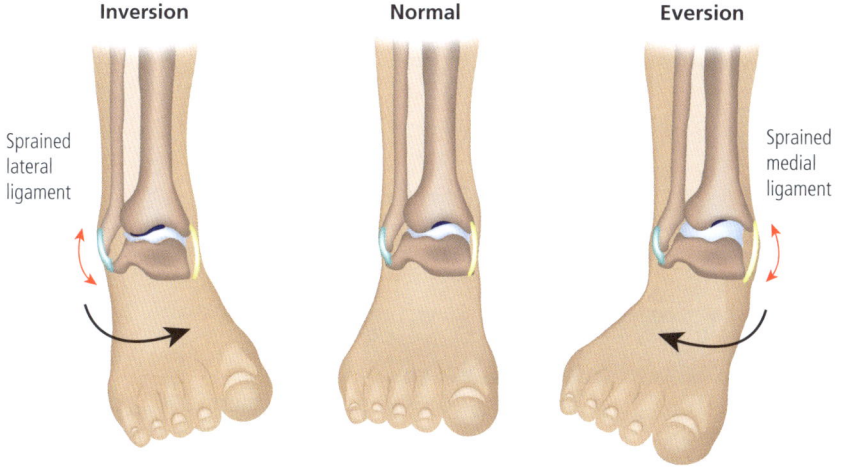

Figure 3.2 Ankle sprains: inversion, normal and eversion

> **Typical mistake**
>
> Do not mix up strain and sprain. A strain is a muscle or tendon injury and a sprain is a ligament injury.

> **Exam tip**
>
> Make sure you can give a sporting example of when a strain and a sprain occurs.

Anterior cruciate ligament (ACL)

The anterior cruciate ligament (ACL) is found on the inside of the knee. It joins the femur (thigh bone) to the tibia (shin bone). The ACL can be stretched, torn or snapped.

+ **Cause:** ACL injuries are common in sport and can happen when:
  + A performer twists their knee, for example, a netball player who lands from jumping to catch the ball and tries to twist to face the direction of their next pass.
  + A quick change in direction takes place when running.
  + A player stops suddenly, for example, running in one direction and then stopping to dodge an opponent to get free in basketball.
  + The knee is overextended, for example, stretching out to make a tackle in football.
  + A collision takes place in contact sports such as rugby, where there is a direct blow to the knee.
+ **Symptoms:** a loud pop, severe pain, inflammation and bruising together with a lack of mobility and the feeling that the knee could give way.
+ **Treatment:** PRICE – see Topic area 4.2.
+ **Reducing risk:** see Topic area 1 (Reducing the risk of sports injuries and dealing with common medical conditions) and Topic area 4 (Reducing risk, treatment and rehabilitation of sports injuries and medical conditions).

> **Anterior cruciate ligament (ACL)** The ligament that runs diagonally in the middle of the knee joining the femur to the tibia in the leg.

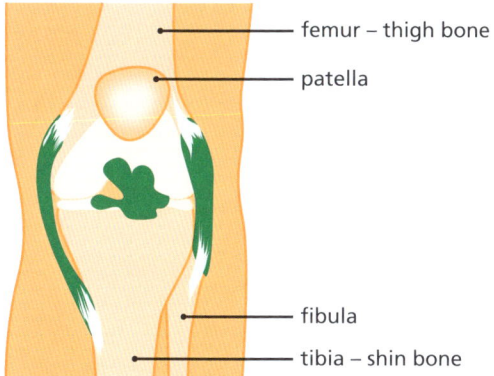

Figure 3.3 Anterior cruciate ligament (ACL)

> **Exam tip**
>
> Make sure you are aware of how to reduce the risk of acute injuries. To help with this look at the causes and also make links with Topic area 1 (Reducing the risk of sports injuries and dealing with common medical conditions).

> **Check your understanding**
>
> 1 Outline the difference between a sprain and a strain.
> 2 Describe what can cause a sprain and a strain when playing sport.
> 3 Identify where the ACL is located in the body.

3.1.5 Skin damage

Playing sport exposes the skin to contact with other surfaces leading to the possibility of injury:
+ Abrasion/grazes.
+ Cuts/lacerations.
+ Contusions (bruises).
+ Blisters.

Table 3.1 Types of skin damage

Injury	Description	Cause – sporting example	Treatment
Abrasion/grazes	Damage to the surface of the skin, for example, the scraping away of a layer of the skin.	Falling onto hard or rough ground such as concrete or by skin rubbing on an artificial surface, for example, falling and sliding on an artificial surface during a hockey match.	Abrasions need to be cleaned and sterilised and then covered with a dressing.
Cuts/lacerations	More severe than an abrasion as the wound is deeper due to the tearing of the skin.	Contact with studs on a football boot or a hockey stick hitting a player and cutting the skin open.	+ Bleeding needs to be stopped by elevating the damaged area and applying pressure. + Then minor cuts should be cleaned, sterilised and covered with a dressing. + Deep lacerations/cuts may need closure with surgical tape, glue or stitches.
Contusion (bruises)	When blood vessels have become damaged, resulting in a bruise.	Contact either with the ground through falling or contact with another player, for example, landing awkwardly after attempting an interception in netball.	Apply PRICE (protection, rest, ice, compression and elevation – see Topic area 4.2.4).
Blisters	Small bags of fluid that develop under the skin to protect damage caused by friction.	Friction caused by poorly fitting footwear or from sports equipment, for example, blisters on the hand from gripping a badminton racket.	Clean and sterilise the area and, in some cases, cover with a dressing.

> **Abrasion** Where the surface of the skin is damaged.
>
> **Cut/laceration** Where the skin tears.
>
> **Contusion** A bruise caused by blood leaking into the area.
>
> **Blisters** Small fluid sacks that are caused by friction.

> **Check your understanding**
>
> 4 Describe a contusion and state **one** cause of it in sport.
> 5 Blisters occur regularly in sport. State **one** cause of blisters and describe the treatment you would give to this injury.

> **Now test yourself**
>
> Identify **two** sporting examples where each of the following injuries could occur: abrasions, cuts, contusions and blisters.
>
> TESTED

Check your understanding and progress at www.hoddereducation.co.uk/myrevisionnotes

3.1.6 Fractures

A break or a crack in a bone is called a fracture. Open and closed fractures are common acute injuries caused by falls or collisions in sport or by being hit with sporting equipment, for example, a hockey stick.

Open

An open fracture is when the soft tissue or skin has been damaged because the bone has moved or broken through the skin. This is more serious as there is a higher risk of infection.

Closed

A closed fracture is a clean break to a bone that does not penetrate through the skin or damage any surrounding tissue.

> **Open fracture** Where a bone is broken and breaks through the skin.
>
> **Closed fracture** Where a bone is broken but there is no break in the skin.

Treatment of fractures

+ A simple fracture needs medical attention. Until the patient arrives at hospital, it is important to keep them comfortable, calm and the injury site still.
+ At hospital, the injury will be assessed using an X-ray (see Topic area 4.2.5) and will be immobilised with a plaster cast or sling and crutches given to ease weight bearing for a lower-body fracture.
+ If necessary, surgery will be carried out to realign or pin bones.
+ Anti-inflammatory and pain relief medication may be prescribed. Physiotherapy may also be needed to improve mobility and strengthen the surrounding connective tissue.

> **Anti-inflammatory medication** Medicine that reduces swelling.
>
> **Dislocation** Where the bones in a joint become separated.
>
> **Joint** Where two or more bones meet.
>
> **Concussion** An injury that occurs when the brain is shaken inside the skull.

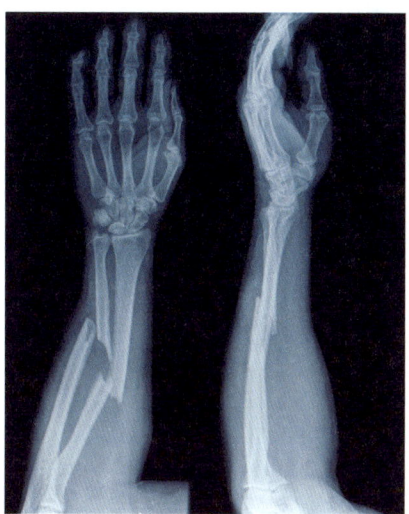

Figure 3.4 X-ray of a fractured forearm

> **Check your understanding**
>
> 6 Outline the difference between an open and closed fracture.

3.1.7 Dislocations

A dislocation is an injury to a joint where the ends of the bones are forced from their normal positions.

+ **Cause:** dislocations can occur as the result of a fall or a collision in sport. They can also occur when the muscles and tendons surrounding the joint are weak.
+ **Treatment:** similar to the treatment of a fracture. Only a medical professional should try to reposition bones. It is important to keep the joint immobilised until medical help arrives.

> **Exam tip**
>
> When asked to explain how an injury can happen, make sure you are specific. For example, saying a bad tackle causes a fracture is too vague. A better answer would be a bad tackle that *causes the performer to fall awkwardly* can cause a fracture.

3.1.8 Head injuries

Head injuries occur when there is damage to the scalp, skull or brain caused by trauma.

Concussion

Concussion can be a very serious brain injury that, for some, can result in fatality.
+ **Cause:** concussion is caused by an impact to the head and is a very common injury in rugby during tackles. The brain is shaken inside the skull and can sometimes result in the loss of consciousness.
+ **Symptoms:** include dizziness, nausea, loss of balance and severe headache.
+ **Treatment:** involves removing the player from the pitch, applying ice and referring them to a qualified healthcare professional. In more serious cases, dial 999. The player will need to rest and be symptom-free for at least one week (or two weeks for under 18s) and only return when authorised by a healthcare professional.

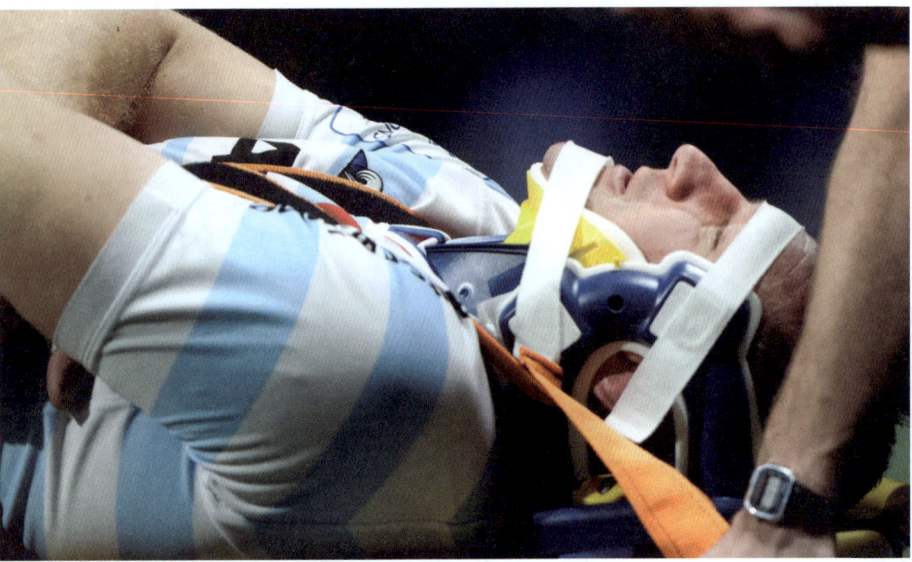

Figure 3.5 A head injury in rugby

Possible links with head injuries and the onset of dementia and Alzheimer's disease

Recent research has shown that there is a link between head injuries and the onset of dementia and Alzheimer's disease.
+ **Dementia:** a group of symptoms associated with a decline in memory, thinking skills and behaviour; it interferes with everyday life.
+ **Alzheimer's disease:** a type of dementia that affects memory, thinking and behaviour.

This link is as a result of receiving repeated blows to the head or repeated concussion. Some contact sports carry a greater risk.
+ In football, for example, collisions occur and a player repeatedly heads the ball.
+ In boxing, competitors receive blows to the head.
+ In rugby, tackles frequently make contact with the head. Consequently, World Rugby has recently introduced the Head Injury Assessment (HIA) protocol to help tackle the issue of concussion in the sport.

> **Dementia** A general term for a decline in mental ability, which affects the ability to perform everyday activities.
>
> **Alzheimer's disease** A type of progressive and irreversible form of dementia that affects memory, thinking and behaviour.

Check your understanding

7 Identify the types of sport that have links with head injuries and the onset of dementia.

Exam tip

Make sure you can link head injuries with types of sporting activities.

3.2 Chronic injuries

REVISED

Chronic injuries are overuse injuries to muscles, tendons, bones and joints.

3.2.1 Overview of chronic injuries

+ They are caused by **overuse**, continuous stress, **repetitive movement** of an area such as the continuous impact of long-distance running on the bones in the legs and feet, or not enough rest.
+ They **develop gradually** over a period of time.
+ They can also keep **reoccurring** and can lead to a gradual loss of function or increase in weakness.
+ Causes:
  + The body can be overloaded too quickly if the appropriate intensity, duration and frequency of activity is not achieved.
  + Poor technique and training can place excessive stress on muscles, tendons and ligaments, as can incorrect equipment and clothing (such as worn-out trainers).
  + Poor core stability and a lack of muscle strength or endurance can also be a cause of chronic injuries.
  + Muscle imbalance (strong tight muscles versus weak stretched muscles) with a lack of flexibility will place added stress on a joint.
  + Finally, biomechanical issues can cause a chronic injury, for example, being flat-footed.
+ Treatment:
  + Most chronic injuries are treated with the PRICE method and rest (see Topic area 4.2.4).
  + Massaging the injured area and stretching and bandaging can also help, together with heat treatment and anti-inflammatory medicines.
  + More serious cases may require an ultrasound and physiotherapy treatment.

> **Chronic injuries** Overuse injuries caused by repetitive movement that places stress on a particular muscle, tendon, ligament, bone or joint.

Check your understanding

8 State which of the following statements are true or false.
   + A chronic injury results in immediate pain.
   + A chronic injury occurs over a long period of time.
   + An open fracture is an example of a chronic injury.

Typical mistake

Sometimes the word chronic can be misleading as it suggests a serious injury that could be life-threatening. Instead, it is an injury that is caused by overuse of a body part.

Exam tip

As well as the causes, symptoms and treatment of chronic injuries, questions could also ask you how to reduce the risks of these injuries.

3.2.2 Tendonitis

Tendonitis is inflammation or irritation of a tendon. If a tendon ruptures due to extreme tendonitis this can result in an acute injury rather than a chronic injury.

+ **Symptoms:** include joint pain, mild swelling, thickness of the tendon, tenderness and stiffness. These symptoms limit the range of motion.
+ **Treatment:** you can treat mild tendon injuries yourself with rest, ice, support and pain medication. However, if it is severe and leads to the rupture of a tendon, surgery may be required.
+ **Reducing risk:** see Topic area 1 (Reducing the risk of sports injuries and dealing with common medical conditions) and Topic area 4 (Reducing risk, treatment and rehabilitation of sports injuries and medical conditions).

Table 3.2 Locations and causes of tendonitis

Tendon	Location	Cause
Achilles tendon	Back of the ankle	Lots of running and jumping. For example, basketball.
Rotator cuff tendons	Shoulder	Repetitive overhead activities such as swimming, throwing and racket strokes.
Patellar tendon	Knee	Often called 'jumper's knee' caused by lots of running and jumping on hard surfaces. For example, triple jump.

> **Tendonitis** Inflammation or irritation of a tendon.
>
> **Achilles tendon** Found at the back of the ankle and connects the calf muscle to the heel bone.
>
> **Rotator cuff tendons** A group of tendons that attach the shoulder muscles to the upper arm (humerus).
>
> **Patellar tendon** Found at the knee and connects the kneecap (patella) to the shin bone (tibia).

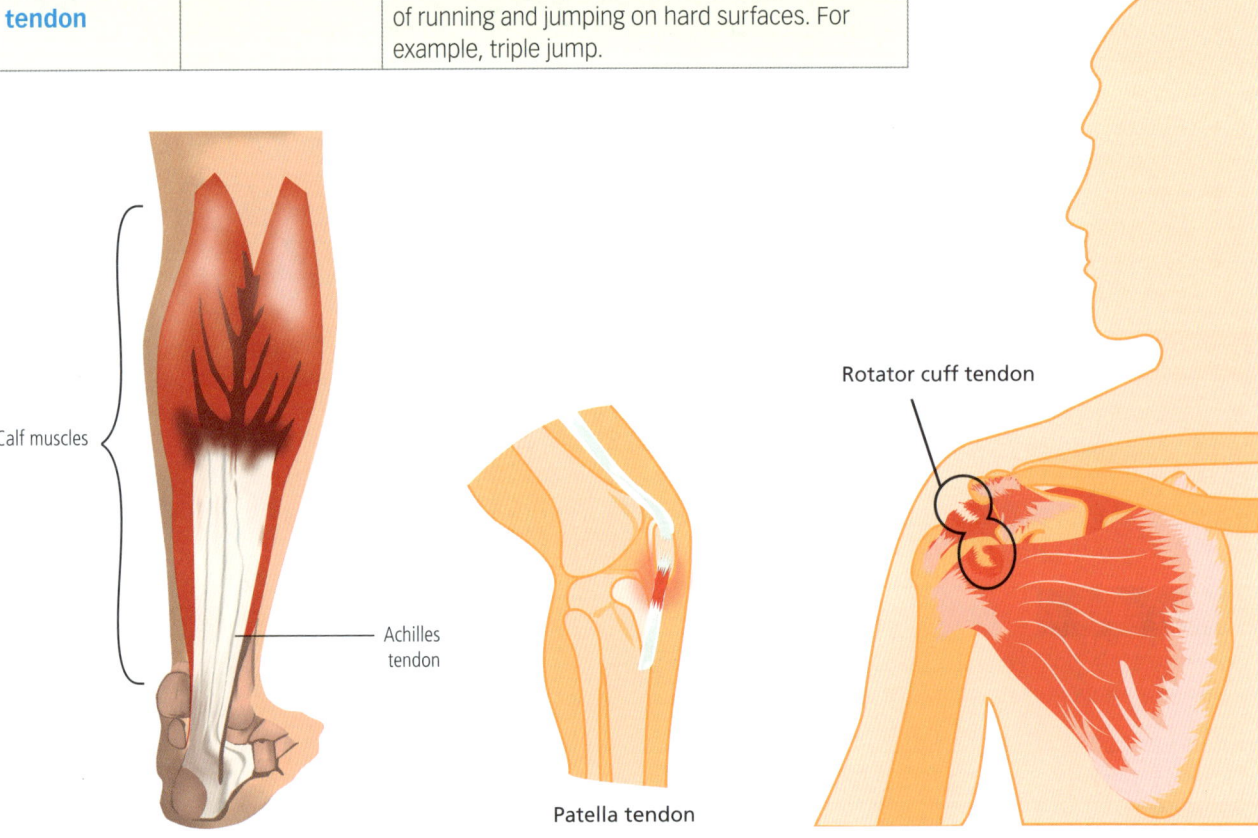

Figure 3.6 Achilles tendon

Figure 3.7 Patella tendon

Figure 3.8 Rotator cuff tendons

> **Now test yourself** — TESTED
>
> There are four tendons listed in this topic: ACL, Achilles, rotator cuff and patellar. List where on the body these tendons are found.

Check your understanding and progress at www.hoddereducation.co.uk/myrevisionnotes

3.2.3 Epicondylitis

The long bones of the body and upper arm have small bumps called **epicondyles** where tendons and ligaments attach to the bone. There are two epicondyles on the humerus (upper arm) near the elbow. **Epicondylitis** is a chronic injury involving the swelling or tearing of the muscles and tendons around the elbow joint.

+ **Cause:** usually caused by repetitive use of the forearm and can last between six months and two years.
+ **Symptoms:** include pain, tenderness and stiffness when trying to move the arm.
+ **Treatment:** involves rest, pain and anti-inflammatory medication together with applying ice to the affected area. More severe cases may require surgery.
+ **Reducing risk:** see Topic area 1 (Reducing the risk of sports injuries and dealing with common medical conditions) and Topic area 4 (Reducing risk, treatment and rehabilitation of sports injuries and medical conditions).

> **Epicondyles** A part that sticks out at the end of a bone where tendons and ligaments attach.
>
> **Epicondylitis** A painful swelling of tendons at the end of a bone.
>
> **Tennis elbow (lateral epicondylitis)** Inflamed tendons that cause pain around the outside of the elbow due to repetitive actions such as tennis strokes.

Lateral epicondylitis (tennis elbow)

With **tennis elbow**, pain is mostly felt where the tendons of the forearm muscles attach to the bony bump on the **outside** of the elbow (lateral epicondylitis). The tendons that are used to straighten the wrist become inflamed and tiny tears occur.

Tennis elbow can be caused by playing racket sports such as tennis, golf or squash, and in particular:

+ the use of poor technique in tennis such as the backhand stroke
+ weak shoulder and wrist muscles
+ using tennis rackets that are too small or too tightly strung
+ hitting heavy, wet balls or hitting the ball off centre on the racket.

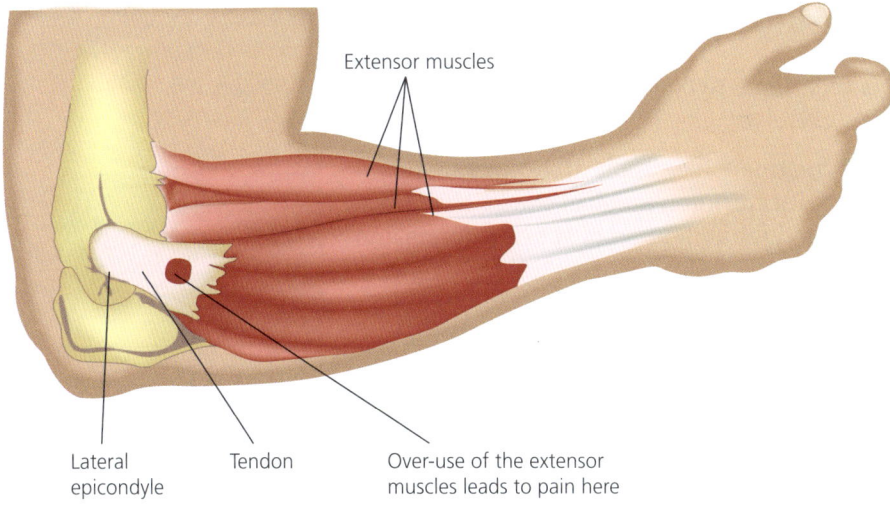

Figure 3.9 Tennis elbow – lateral epicondylitis

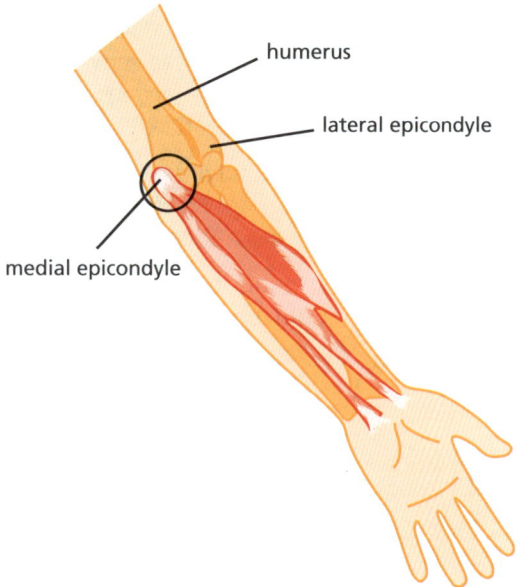

Figure 3.10 Golfer's elbow – medial epicondylitis

Medial epicondylitis (golfer's elbow)

With golfer's elbow, pain is mostly felt where the tendons of the forearm muscles attach to the bony bump on the **inside** of the elbow (medial epicondyle).

Golfer's elbow can occur due to repetition of the swinging arm in the following sports:
+ **Racket sports:** improper technique with racket strokes, for example, the backhand in tennis, using excessive topspin or using a racket that is too small or heavy.
+ **Throwing sports:** improper throwing technique, for example, football and javelin.
+ **Weight training:** using improper technique to lift weights, for example, curling the wrists during a biceps exercise.

For information on reducing risk and treatment, see Topic area 1 (Reducing the risk of sports injuries and dealing with common medical conditions) and Topic area 4 (Reducing risk, treatment and rehabilitation of sports injuries and medical conditions).

3.2.4 Shin splints

Shin splints (medial tibial stress syndrome) typically occur after physical activity when the tendons that connect the muscles to the tibia (shin bone) become inflamed.
+ **Cause:** shin splints often occur as a result of repeatedly putting weight on the legs through lots of running and jumping. It is a common condition with long-distance runners and dancers and performers who have suddenly changed their training routines. Other factors include having flat feet or rigid arches and exercising with improper or worn-out footwear.
+ **Symptoms:** pain and tenderness along the inside edge of the tibia; mild swelling may occur in the area. This can last a few weeks.
+ **Treatment:** includes rest, applying ice, pain and anti-inflammatory medication, wearing an elastic compression bandage to prevent further swelling and supportive shoes with good cushioning. If you continue to exercise, it is important to warm up thoroughly, stretch and try to exercise on soft ground.
+ **Reducing risk:** see Topic area 1 (Different factors which influence the risk and severity of injury) 1.1.4 (Footwear) and 1.2.1 (Technique ability) and Topic area 4 (Reducing risk, treatment and rehabilitation of sports injuries and medical conditions).

> **Golfer's elbow (medial epicondylitis)** Inflamed tendons that cause pain around the inside of the elbow.

> **Typical mistake**
> Do not make the mistake of naming an injury in your answer, which is already named in the question. For example, naming muscle strain when it is already mentioned in a question.
>
> Remember, tennis elbow occurs on the outside of the elbow and golfer's elbow on the inside.

> **Shin splints (medial tibial stress syndrome)** Pain along the shin bone (tibia) caused by exercise.

Check your understanding and progress at www.hoddereducation.co.uk/myrevisionnotes

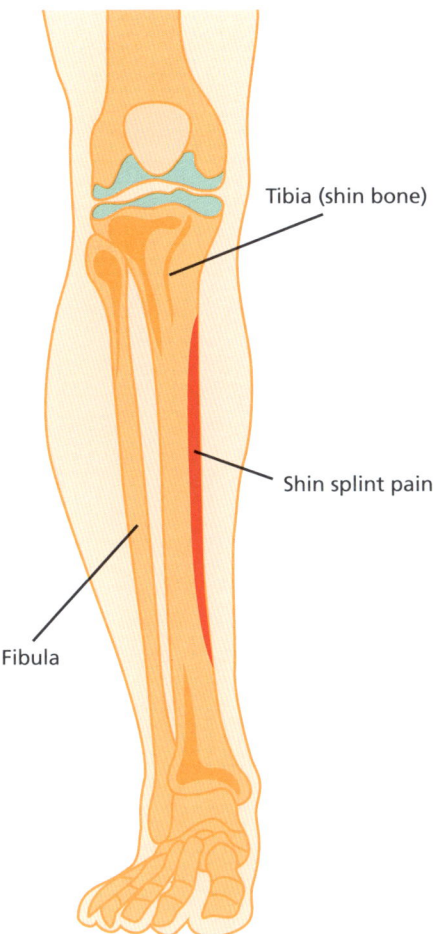

Figure 3.11 Shin splints – medial tibial stress syndrome

3.2.5 Stress fractures

A stress fracture can be classed as both an acute injury (see Topic area 3.1) or a chronic injury (see Topic area 3.2). It is a very small crack in a bone. It usually happens through repetitive trauma and is common in bones of the lower leg or foot. It is common in long-distance runners who put their legs and feet under stress through repeated impact. A stress fracture can also occur with overtraining, changing the surface a performer exercises on – for example, from grass to concrete – or through incorrect training or technique.

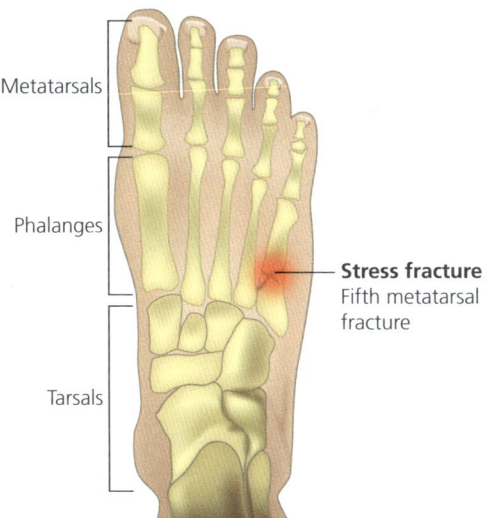

Figure 3.12 A stress fracture of the foot

Now test yourself

State **one** example of another sport (not tennis or golf) in which Achilles tendonitis, shin splints, golfer's elbow and tennis elbow can occur.

TESTED

Check your understanding

9 Explain the difference between acute and chronic injuries. State **two** examples of each.

10 A physiotherapist has diagnosed shin splints. Identify this type of injury and describe what treatment could be used to help recovery.

Stress fracture A very small crack in a bone caused by overuse or repetitive force.

Exam tip

You need to be able to explain how to reduce the risk of each injury and also describe the relevant treatment. To do this you need to make links with Topic area 1 (Different factors which influence the risk and severity of injury) and Topic area 4 (Reducing risk, treatment and rehabilitation of sports injuries and medical conditions).

Check your understanding

11 Describe how a runner can reduce the risk of a stress fracture.

Exam checklist

In this section, you learned about different types of sports injuries and their causes.

In 3.1, the **acute injuries** were:
+ Soft tissue and hard tissue injuries.
+ Strains of muscles and tendons.
+ Ligament sprains.
+ Skin damage injuries such as abrasions/grazes, cuts/lacerations, contusions (bruises) and blisters.
+ Open and closed fractures.
+ Dislocations.
+ Head injuries including concussion and possible links with head injuries and the onset of dementia and Alzheimer's disease.

In 3.2, the **chronic injuries** were:
+ Tendonitis of the Achilles tendon in the ankle, the rotator cuff tendons in the shoulder and the patellar tendon in the knee.
+ Epicondylitis of the outside of the elbow (tennis elbow) and inside of the elbow (golfer's elbow).
+ Shin splints.
+ Stress fractures.

Exam-style questions

1 Copy and complete the table below stating whether each type of injury is either acute or chronic. [4]

Injury type	Acute or chronic
Tendonitis	
Concussion	
Ankle sprain	
Abrasion	

2 ACL injuries are very common in netball. Explain **two** ways in which an ACL injury can be caused during a match. [2]

3 State **three** examples of chronic injuries. [3]

4 Match up the type of injury to a suitable example. [3]

Type of injury		Example
Abrasion		Bruise
Contusion		Graze
Laceration		Deep cut

5 Other than a fracture, identify **three** different types of injury that can occur at the knee. [3]

6 State a cause and treatment for each of the following injuries: [4]

	Cause	Treatment
Muscle strain		
Concussion		

7 Describe tendonitis and identify **two** symptoms associated with tendonitis. [3]

8 Using a sporting example, describe how tendonitis can occur at the shoulder joint. [1]

9 State the type of injury that is linked to the onset of dementia and Alzheimer's disease. [1]

10 Identify the part of the body where a sports performer would experience an epicondylitis injury. [1]

Choose the correct answer.
a Elbow
b Foot
c Knee
d Shoulder

11 State **three** ways in which a performer can reduce the risk of a chronic injury. [3]

12 Identify the **two** types of fracture that are acute injuries and, using a practical example from a contact sport, explain how these fractures can occur. [6]

Check your understanding and progress at www.hoddereducation.co.uk/myrevisionnotes

Topic area 4: Reducing risk, treatment and rehabilitation of sports injuries and medical conditions

4.1 Measures that can be taken before and during participation in sport or physical activity to reduce risk and severity of injury/medical conditions

REVISED

There are a number of measures that can be taken before and during participation in sport or physical activity that can reduce risk and the severity of injury/medical conditions. These are:
+ safety checks
+ strategies to reduce the risk of sports injuries and medical conditions
+ emergency action plans (EAPs).

> **Risk** A possibility of injury.

4.1.1 Safety checks

Safety checks must be carried out before a sporting activity, but should also be ongoing throughout. Safety checks before an activity include checking a playing surface for any harmful debris such as glass, checking players for suitable clothing and footwear and checking the area around the performance area, for example, post padding in netball or benches and bags around the edge of a sports hall.

Risk assessments

A risk assessment is a written document that identifies any possible hazards and proposes ways to remove or reduce the risk of harm occurring. It is written by someone who has the relevant knowledge, experience and skills, such as a coach. Carrying out a risk assessment minimises the chances of injuries occurring by making equipment, the performer and the performance area safe.
+ Any possible hazards or risks that can cause injury are identified, then evaluated.
+ If the risk is too high, a decision is taken on whether the sporting activity can take place.
+ A risk assessment will identify which players could become injured and how.
+ It enables the supervisor to take the necessary steps to minimise or eliminate risks, for example, calling off a game of rugby if the pitch is frozen.

> **Risk assessment** Identifies the possible hazards or risks that can cause injury and how to avoid them.
>
> **Hazards** An unsafe condition that can cause injury.

Level of risk

The level of the hazard should also be assessed as low, medium or high. For example, not doing a warm-up would be low risk, a player colliding with another player could be classed as medium risk and a player slipping on a wet surface and fracturing a bone on impact would be classed as high risk.

Risk Assessment					
Potential hazard	Who is at risk?	Existing control measures	Risk rating	Preventative measures	Responsibilities

Figure 4.1 A typical risk-assessment template

Control measures for the removal of hazards and reduction of risks

A control measure is something that is put in place to remove a hazard or reduce a risk. For example, a control measure to reduce the risk of a player slipping on the court would be to ensure appropriate footwear is worn or to check the ground for any spillages and clean them up. Control measures must be carried out before and during a sporting activity to ensure all hazards are removed and any risk reduced.

Before an activity, control measures should include:
+ checking the playing surface for harmful debris such as wet leaves and glass
+ checking the area around the pitch for fencing and boards, padding on posts and ensuring corner flags are secure
+ checking players for suitable clothing, footwear, jewellery, loose hair, etc.

During the activity, checks should be made constantly and include:
+ checking the weather throughout. If it deteriorates and is no longer safe, the outdoor activity should be stopped
+ checking to ensure that players are coping with the level of the game and that there are no medical issues. For example, a coach should be aware of any asthma sufferers on their team and visually check their breathing while playing.

Exam tip
Make sure you can explain how a risk assessment can help to reduce the risk and severity of injury and give sporting examples.

Characteristics of the individual/group

It is important that the characteristics of an individual or group involved in the activity are considered, to ensure safe practice:
+ **Age of the participants** – young children often require more supervision as they can become excited and may not pay attention.
+ **Individual fitness levels** – members of the group who are not as fit as others could face a greater risk of injury if they try to push themselves too hard.
+ **Experience of the participants** – an experienced performer will participate in a more demanding session so the risk of injury could be higher. For example, in cricket, the ball will be bowled much faster, therefore increasing the risk of injury.
+ **Any medical conditions participants may have** – such as asthma or diabetes (see Topic area 5 – Causes, symptoms and treatment of medical conditions).

Check your understanding and progress at www.hoddereducation.co.uk/myrevisionnotes

Group size

The size of a group needs to be considered in a risk assessment, as a large group of players on court can lead to injuries through collisions or there could be a lot of noise, making it difficult to hear instructions.

> **Now test yourself** — TESTED
>
> Using a sport/activity that you take part in, create a list of **five** risks and state a control measure for each risk.

> **Check your understanding**
>
> 1 Explain why it is important to carry out a risk assessment for a sporting activity.
> 2 Identify **three** things that a supervisor should check before a football match on an outdoor pitch.

4.1.2 Strategies to help reduce the risk of sports injuries and medical conditions

A strategy is a plan of action that can help to prevent an injury before it actually happens.

Medicals can help to find out whether an individual has a high risk of a health problem (mental or physical). They can also be used to detect a medical condition early before any symptoms occur and potentially save lives.

Screening

In sport, screening can be used to reduce injury and involves assessing:
+ muscle imbalances
+ core strength
+ range of joint movement
+ postural alignment
+ mobility.

If any problems are detected, a specific training programme can be followed for improvement, thus reducing the chance of a potential injury and at the same time enhancing performance. For example, many young elite performers have CRY heart screening. CRY stands for 'cardiac risk in the young' and an electrocardiogram (ECG) is used to assess and monitor a performer's heart. This test is encouraged by most sports governing bodies due to the demands of elite sport and the stress it can place on the heart.

National Governing Body (NGB) policies

Each governing body of sport will have specific controls and regulations to reduce the risk of injury. For example, England Squash state that eye protection should be worn by all junior players at all England Squash competitions and activities. The Football Association (FA) has a policy that shin pads must be worn.

4.1.3 Emergency action plans (EAPs)

An emergency action plan (EAP) is a written plan detailing what action and procedures need to be followed in the event of an emergency such as an injury at matches and training sessions. It ensures the safety of performers, enables supervisors to know what to do when dealing with an emergency and therefore reduces the risk of serious injuries occurring that could be life-threatening.

Strategy A plan of action.

Medicals An examination by a doctor to assess a person's physical health and fitness.

Screening Identifies the current medical condition of an individual to determine whether there is a risk of complications from exercise.

CRY An abbreviation for 'cardiac risk in the young'.

ECG Stands for an electrocardiogram machine. Electrodes are placed onto the player's chest and the wires connect to an ECG machine and a printout is produced of the heart's electrical activity.

Emergency action plan (EAP) A written plan detailing what action and procedures need to be followed in the event of an emergency.

An EAP has three main sections:
+ emergency personnel
+ emergency communication
+ emergency equipment.

Emergency personnel
In the event of an emergency, it is important to know who to contact and how. Emergency personnel includes details of the first responder, qualified first aider, the coach, and in some venues the doctor/nurse.

Emergency communication
The EAP needs to contain details of contact numbers for the emergency services (999) and the location of the nearest telephone. In sport, mobile phones are often not as accessible.

Emergency equipment
Details of the location of emergency equipment must be included on the EAP. A first aid kit, evacuation chair, wheelchair, stretcher, defibrillator, inhaler and ice packs are all examples of emergency equipment.

Emergency Action Plan
If an athlete has a life-threatening emergency, one person should stay with them and call 999.

Information for the dispatcher:
Indicate your need for an ambulance
Current location's address: _____
Your call back number: _____

Injured person's approximate age and medical issue (e.g. head injury, spine injury, heart condition).

Directions for first responders to find the entrance to the facility and find the injured person.

A second person should be waiting at the entrance to help first responders locate the injured person.

This person should also call the injured athlete's emergency contact number (if they are not already present).

A third person should serve as a 'runner' to retrieve medical and first-aid supplies as needed for the person who is attending to the injured athlete.

A fourth person should take responsibility for any other people present in the facility and ensure that the area around the injured person is clear.

Address of nearest hospital: _____
Phone number of hospital: _____

Figure 4.2 Emergency Action Plan

Now test yourself TESTED

Create your own EAP for a sporting activity at your local club, leisure centre or school.

Check your understanding

3 An emergency action plan (EAP) has three main components. Identify the **three** components and give an example for each one.

> **Exam tip**
>
> Questions on EAPs will require knowledge of the three components and examples from each.

> **Typical mistake**
>
> Make sure you fully explain your answer. For example, with emergency communication, say why you are dialling 999.

> **Typical mistake**
>
> Do not confuse a risk assessment with an emergency action plan (EAP). A risk assessment identifies possible hazards and how to avoid them, whereas an EAP describes what measures should be taken following an injury.

Check your understanding and progress at www.hoddereducation.co.uk/myrevisionnotes

4.2 Responses and treatment to injuries and medical conditions in a sporting context

REVISED

There are many different types of injury that can occur when playing sport so there are different responses that need to be made depending on the severity of the injury. Treatment will also differ from simple ice by a first aider to medical intervention by a trained professional at hospital.

4.2.1 SALTAPS on-field assessment routine (See, Ask, Look, Touch, Active, Passive, Strength)

The use of SALTAPS as an on-field injury assessment routine is used to assess whether a player should continue in the activity after an injury. It has the advantage of being a quick and easy procedure to follow.

SALTAPS is an acronym for the steps that should be followed to assess the seriousness of an injury.

- **See** – stop the game when a player is injured, ask what happened and observe the injury.
- **Ask** – questions about the injury, for example, where does it hurt? How did it happen?
- **Look** – at the injury site for bruising, bleeding, swelling or deformity.
- **Touch** – the area gently to feel for swelling, deformity, heat, lumps or bumps.
- **Active movement** – check whether the performer can move the injured area without too much pain.
- **Passive movement** – here the assessor moves the injured body part to see how much pain can be felt by the casualty.
- **Strength testing** – find out whether the performer can stand, lift or put pressure on the injured area and ask whether they feel able to continue.

> **SALTAPS** An acronym for the steps that should be followed to assess the seriousness of an injury: See, Ask, Look, Touch, Active movement, Passive movement and Strength testing.
>
> **DRABC** An acronym for the steps that should be followed when initially attending to an injury: Danger, Response, Airway, Breathing and Circulation.
>
> **Circulation** Where the heart pumps blood around the body.

Now test yourself — TESTED

Using role play, practise on a friend the steps you need to follow to assess an injury.

4.2.2 DRABC (Danger, Response, Airway, Breathing, Circulation)

DRABC is an acronym for the procedure that should be followed when attending an injury to find out if it is life-threatening: Danger, Response, Airway, Breathing and Circulation.

With an injured participant, the nominated first aider needs to do an initial DRABC procedure in the following order:

- **Danger** – it is very important to check whether there is any danger in getting to a casualty, for example, are they in a safe place.
- **Response** – the first aider then needs to see if the patient responds to a command or pain, for example, with a pinch of the earlobe.
- **Airway** – then they need to check that the airway is clear by opening the mouth.
- **Breathing** – then they need to check that the patient is breathing normally by listening for sounds of breathing and seeing if their chest moves.
- **Circulation** – finally, they should check for signs of severe bleeding.

The advantages of DRABC are that using an acronym makes it easier to remember each stage. It also enables life-threatening information to be collected quickly.

> **Typical mistake**
>
> Learn the steps carefully and in order. 'S' for see also has the word 'stop' in its explanation, so it is easy to muddle the two if learned out of context.

4.2.3 Recovery position

Following application of the DRABC procedure, it is important to place the casualty in the recovery position. This position is used for unconscious performers who are breathing and have no other life-threatening conditions. Placing a patient in the recovery position will keep an airway clear and open so they do not choke on vomit and also prevents the tongue dropping back and blocking the airway. Figure 4.3 illustrates and explains the recovery position.

Recovery position A position used to keep an airway clear and open in an unconscious patient.

1 Open the casualty's airway by gently tilting their head back and lifting their chin.

2 Straighten the casualty's limbs.

3 Put the casualty's arm nearest to you out at right angles to their body, with the elbow bent and the palm facing up.

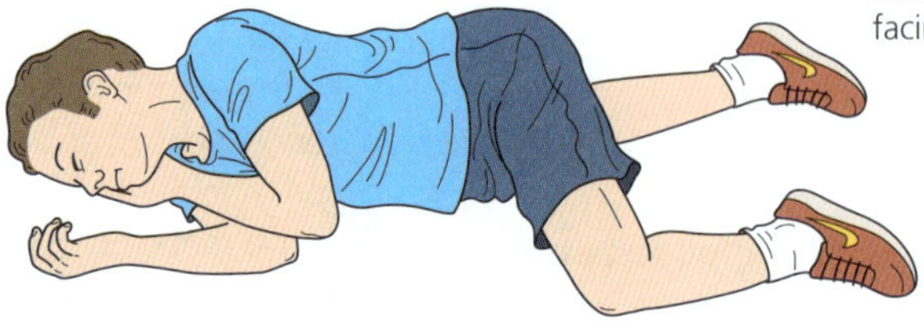

4 Take hold of the casualty's other hand and put the back of it against their opposite cheek – hold it there.

5 With your other hand, take hold of the casualty's far leg, just above the knee, and pull it up until the foot is flat on the floor.

6 Keeping their hand pressed against their cheek, gently roll the casualty towards you onto their side, using the knee as leverage.

Figure 4.3 The recovery position

> **Now test yourself** — TESTED
>
> Practise placing a partner into the recovery position. Use the following link to help you if necessary. www.nhs.uk/conditions/first-aid/recovery-position

4.2.4 PRICE therapy (Protection, Rest, Ice, Compress, Elevate)

PRICE therapy is used for two or three days for acute but less serious soft tissue injuries to reduce blood flow, swelling and ease pain. A soft tissue injury results in bleeding which causes swelling, pain and scar tissue.

+ **Protection** – the affected area should be protected from further injury. This can be achieved by using a support, for example.
+ **Rest** – it is important to rest the injury immediately to avoid making it worse.
+ **Ice** – the injured area needs to be cooled to cause the contraction of blood vessels and thereby restrict blood flow in that area. This results in less swelling and a faster recovery. Ice packs should be applied to the area for at least ten minutes to achieve this.
+ **Compression** – bandaging the injury reduces swelling and gives support.
+ **Elevation** – keeping the injured area above the level of the heart reduces blood flow, which helps to prevent swelling.

PRICE An acronym for dealing with acute soft tissue injuries: Protection, Rest, Ice, Compression and Elevation.

IMPORTANT NOTE: PRICE should only be used for acute soft tissue injuries. It is not suitable for injuries where there is a risk of infection or heavy blood loss. It should also not be used where it could make pain worse by applying it. Applying PRICE to a serious injury wastes time when the injured person should be taken directly to hospital.

Figure 4.4 PRICE therapy

> **Exam tip**
>
> Do not just learn what the acronyms SALTAPS, DRABC and PRICE mean – make sure you can apply them to a context.

Check your understanding

4 Identify the stage of the SALTAPS on-field assessment routine that the following statements explain.
   + Checking for bleeding, bruising, swelling or deformity.
   + Examining the injured area for pain and tenderness.
5 Explain the difference between 'active' and 'passive' for the on-field assessment of SALTAPS.
6 State how long you would apply the PRICE procedure to an injury.

4.2.5 Use of X-rays to detect injury

An X-ray uses images to diagnose and locate:
+ dislocations and fractures
+ other bone conditions such as infections, arthritis or bone cancer
+ foreign objects, enabling their removal.

They take place in a hospital and are a quick and easy way for a doctor to assess the damage and provide the relevant treatment.

> **X-ray** Uses images to see where a bone is fractured or dislocated.

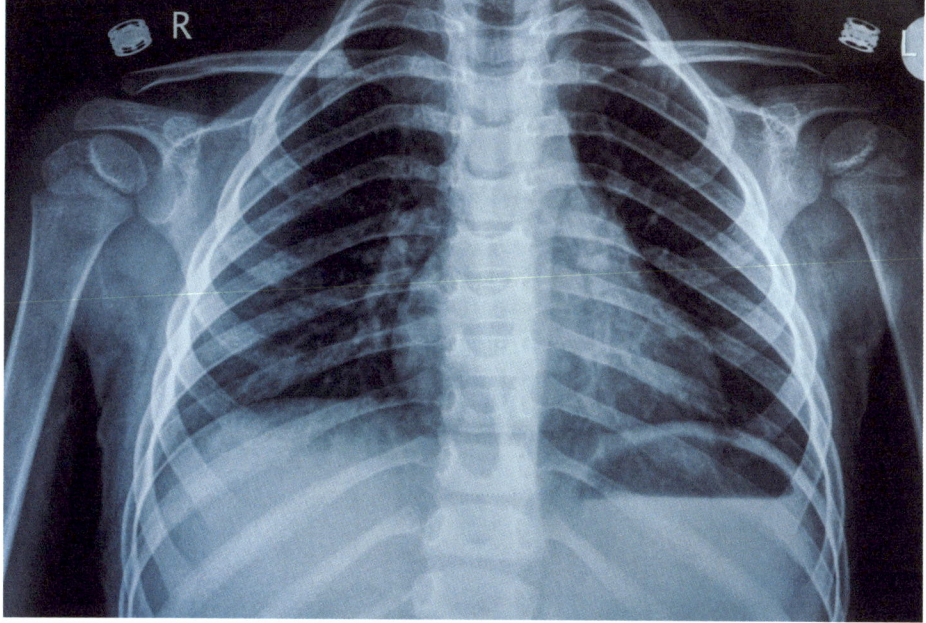

Figure 4.5 An X-ray of the chest

4.2.6 Overview of treatment/therapies

There are a number of different treatments/therapies available for sports injuries. Which one is used can depend on injury type, location and severity. Access also has to be considered as some of these treatments incur costs.

+ Massage.
+ Ultrasound.
+ Electrotherapy.
+ Hydrotherapy.
+ Cryotherapy.
+ Contrast therapy.
+ Painkillers.
+ Support.
+ Immobilisation.

> **Massage** Using hands or massage guns to rub and knead muscles and joints to relieve pain and tension.
>
> **Ultrasound** A medical test that uses high-frequency sound waves to create a live image of the injury inside your body.
>
> **Electrotherapy** The application of an electric current to the injury to accelerate healing and reduce pain and swelling.

Table 4.1 Treatments/therapies

Treatment/therapy	Explanation
Massage	Good for most soft tissue injuries and is usually performed after strenuous activity. + It improves circulation by increasing blood flow, which moves fluid and nutrients through damaged tissue, encouraging healing and accelerating the removal of waste products. + Scar tissue is broken down and it helps muscles to relax and relieves tension. + It can also be used to manage pain and relieve **DOMS** (**d**elayed **o**nset of **m**uscle **s**oreness).
Ultrasound	+ Uses high-frequency sound waves to create an image of the injured part of the body. + This allows a medical professional to assess the damage and decide how to treat the injury.
Electrotherapy	+ Applies an electric current to the injured site to accelerate healing and reduce swelling and pain.
Hydrotherapy	+ Takes place in warm water and is used to improve blood circulation, relieve pain and relax muscles. Exercises include squats, lunges, walking and running. + The buoyancy of the water helps to support body weight. This reduces the load on joints and therefore allows for more exercise than is permitted on land. + Exercising against the resistance of the water helps to strengthen the injured area.
Cryotherapy	+ Use of cold temperatures to treat injuries. + Treating an injury such as a sprain, strain and bruising with ice for 10–20 minutes every two hours has an **analgesic** effect (lowers pain) and can limit swelling by causing **vasoconstriction** of blood vessels (making them smaller), decreasing blood flow to the injured area. + As well as applying ice packs, another cold treatment method is a freeze spray.
Contrast therapy	+ Alternates cold and heat therapy, which will increase blood flow and decrease swelling and pain after exercise, but this should only take place several days after the injury has happened. + Cold therapy is explained in cryotherapy above and heat therapy uses heat to reduce muscle tension, stiffness and pain. It causes **vasodilation** of blood vessels (making them bigger), increasing blood flow and the healing response to a damaged area. + Methods of heat treatment include heat pads, deep heat cream, hot water bottles, heat lamps, heat caused by friction during massage and a hot bath. However, heat treatment should not be used until 72 hours after an injury and when the swelling has reduced.
Painkillers	+ Medicines that reduce pain. + For example, **Ibuprofen** can be taken for pain relief. It is also an anti-inflammatory drug, which means it can reduce swelling.
Support (kinesiology taping/neoprene/bandaging)	+ **Kinesiology taping** provides support and keeps muscles and joints in place to reduce mobility, therefore reducing pain. + **Neoprene** is often used in sport to support an injury and provide compression. + **Bandaging** prevents swelling by reducing blood flow to the injured area. For abrasions and blisters, it can stop bleeding and prevent infection. Bandaging can also be used for support or to hold an ice pack in place.
Immobilisation (cast/splint/sling)	+ **Casts**, **splints** and **slings immobilise** and protect the injured site and hold the injury in place, keeping it secure. They relieve pain and reduce the stress around the injured part. + A splint and sling can be used to elevate the injury to reduce swelling and promote the correct healing position.

Check your understanding and progress at www.hoddereducation.co.uk/myrevisionnotes

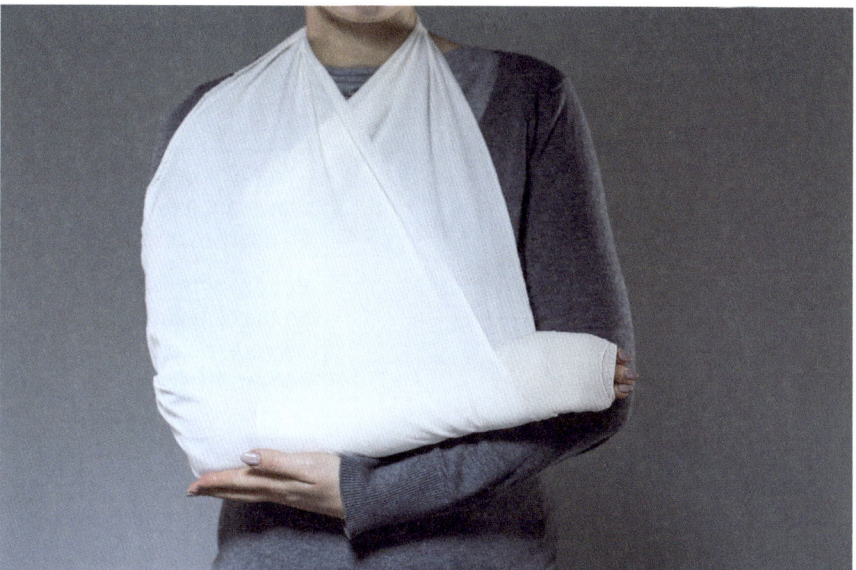

Figure 4.6 Arm sling

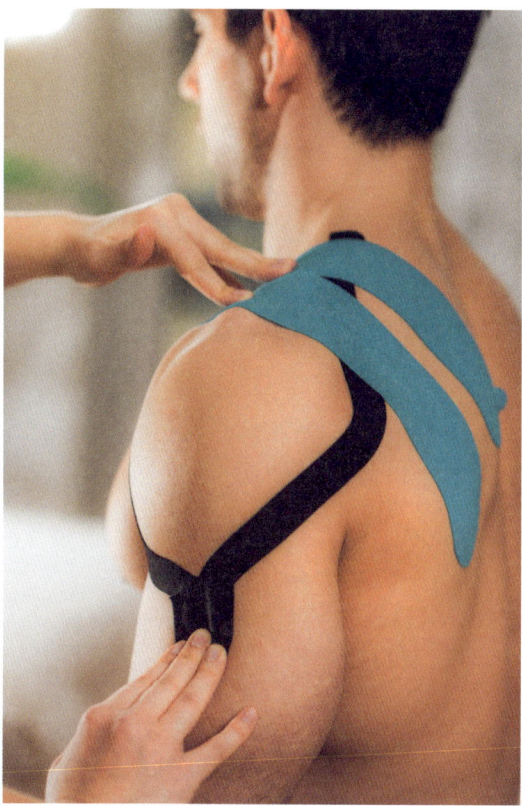

Figure 4.7 Kinesiology taping for shoulder pain

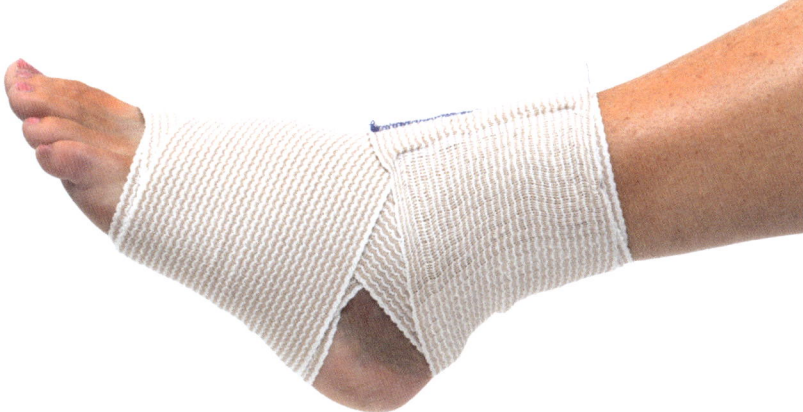

Figure 4.8 Bandaging

DOMS (delayed onset of muscle soreness) Acronym for **d**elayed **o**nset of **m**uscle **s**oreness. Muscles are sore 24–48 hours after exercise.

Hydrotherapy The use of water in the treatment of injuries.

Cryotherapy The use of cold temperatures to treat an injury.

Analgesic A medicine that relieves pain.

Vasoconstriction The narrowing of a blood vessel to reduce blood flow.

Contrast therapy Alternating hot and cold temperatures.

Vasodilation The widening of a blood vessel to increase blood flow.

Painkillers Medication that reduces pain.

Ibuprofen An anti-inflammatory drug that also relieves pain.

Support Something that keeps a joint in place.

Kinesiology tape Tape that provides support and keeps muscles and joints in place to reduce mobility, therefore reducing pain.

Neoprene A synthetic rubber material that supports and compresses an injury.

Bandaging A protective strip of material on an injury.

Immobilisation Keeping the injury still.

Cast A stiff bandage to immobilise and protect an injury.

Splint A hard piece of medical equipment that protects and immobilises an injury.

> **Now test yourself** TESTED
>
> State **five** injuries and for each of these give the appropriate treatment method(s).

> **Exam tip**
>
> For each of these treatments and therapies, make sure you can give examples and explain the benefits of each. Make sure you are aware of the different times when each treatment should be used.

> **Check your understanding**
>
> 7 Describe how massage and splints can help in the treatment of sports injuries. State **two** examples for each.
> 8 Identify **two** methods which use heat to treat sporting injuries.
> 9 State **two** reasons why a sports performer would use hydrotherapy in the treatment of their injury.
> 10 Explain the term cryotherapy.

Sling A piece of material that supports and immobilises an injury.

Endorphins Chemicals produced naturally by the nervous system to help us cope with pain and stress and that boost happiness.

4.2.7 Different psychological effects of dealing with injuries and medical conditions including treatment and long-term rehabilitation

Injuries and medical conditions can prevent an individual from exercising. This can lead to several emotional responses such as sadness, frustration, depression, lack of motivation, anxiety and tension (see more detail in Topic area 1.2.2 – psychological factors). An injured individual may also experience sleep disturbance and alterations in appetite.

Exercise is often done to relieve stress and anxiety because it releases endorphins which are 'feel good' chemicals. No exercise means these chemicals will not be released and stress and anxiety can build up. There are also mental strategies (see Topic area 1.2.4 – mental strategies) that could help overcome any negative psychological effects such as imagery of injury recovery.

Treatment and long-term rehabilitation can also lead to feelings of frustration if there are delays in recovery. Some treatments may also be painful and lead to feelings of anxiety before each visit to a specialist.

> **Exam checklist**
>
> In 4.1, you learned about reducing the risk and severity of injury/medical conditions before and during participation in sport by using:
> + safety checks
> + strategies such as medicals, screening and NGB policies
> + the use of emergency action plans (EAPs).
>
> In 4.2, you learned about responses and treatments to injuries and medical conditions:
>
> + using SALTAPS, DRABC, the recovery position and PRICE therapy
> + the use of X-rays to detect injuries
> + different treatments and therapies: massage, ultrasound, electrotherapy, hydrotherapy, cryotherapy, contrast therapy, painkillers, support and immobilisation
> + the psychological effects of dealing with an injury, its treatment and long-term rehabilitation.

Check your understanding and progress at www.hoddereducation.co.uk/myrevisionnotes

Exam-style questions

1. Identify **one** control measure to prevent injuries caused by the playing surface. [1]

2. State **two** characteristics of a group that a coach will need to take account of to ensure safe practice. [2]

3. Draw **two** lines to match up when the following treatments should be carried out: [2]

Contrast therapy		After activity
Massage		Two or three days later

4. SALTAPS is used to help remember the steps of an on-field injury assessment routine. State the words that the letters 'L' and 'T' stand for. [2]

5. DRABC is an acronym for an on-field injury procedure. Fill in the missing words. [2]

   D = danger
   R = _____
   A = airway
   B = _____
   C = circulation

6. Explain when you would put an injured player into the recovery position. [1]

7. State **two** reasons why you should use PRICE for a soft tissue injury. [2]

8. State **two** reasons why you would not use PRICE in the treatment of an injury. [2]

9. State **two** reasons why bandaging might be used to treat an injury. [2]

10. Which of the following statements is correct? [1]

    Choose the correct answer.

    a Cryotherapy is the use of hot followed by cold temperatures.

    b Electrotherapy uses high-frequency sound waves on an injured site.

    c Hydrotherapy takes place in water.

    d Ultrasound uses an electrical current on the injured site.

11. Following a sports injury, discuss how different treatments and therapies can be used for rehabilitation. [8]

    Your answer should include:
    + Explanation of the different treatment/therapies.
    + Examples of sporting injuries.
    + How each treatment/therapy can rehabilitate the injury.

Topic area 5: Causes, symptoms and treatment of medical conditions

The medical conditions you will study in this topic are:
- Asthma
- Diabetes
- Epilepsy
- Sudden cardiac arrest
- Hypothermia
- Heat exhaustion
- Dehydration.

5.1 Asthma

REVISED

Asthma is a lung condition in which the airways narrow and swell which makes breathing difficult and may trigger coughing, a wheezing sound when breathing out and shortness of breath.

Asthma often starts in childhood and can affect people of all ages. It is a minor inconvenience for some people but for others, it can be a major issue that interferes with daily life and could lead to a life-threatening asthma attack. There is currently no cure for asthma but there are treatments that can keep symptoms under control so that the life of a performer is not detrimentally affected.

> **Asthma** A lung condition in which the airways narrow and swell, making breathing difficult.
>
> **Inhaler** A device that allows medicine to be breathed in to relieve asthma symptoms.

5.1.1 Asthma and exercise

Exercise helps asthma sufferers because it has benefits for the heart and lungs. However, it is important to manage asthma during exercise. Asthma sufferers should ensure:
- They use their medications before exercising to prevent asthma attacks.
- They avoid exercising when they have colds or feel unwell.
- They have their inhaler with them. This is a device that lets the individual breathe in medicine to relieve asthma symptoms.
- They inform the person in charge of the activity so that they can recognise the symptoms and carry out the appropriate treatment in the event of an asthma attack.

Figure 5.1 An athlete with asthma may need to use an inhaler

Check your understanding and progress at www.hoddereducation.co.uk/myrevisionnotes

- They do both a warm-up and cool down and if the weather is cold exercise indoors or wear a mask over their nose and mouth.
- They choose a suitable sport. Sports requiring short bursts of energy, such as football, are better than those requiring endurance, such as running.

> **Triggers** Things that make the onset of a medical condition more likely.
>
> **Nebuliser** A machine that allows high doses of asthma medicine to be breathed in as a mist through a facemask or mouthpiece.

Table 5.1 Overview of asthma

Causes/Triggers	Common symptoms	Treatment
The causes of asthma vary from person to person. It is probably caused by a combination of environmental and genetic/inherited factors. **Environmental factors** that can **trigger** asthma include: - Allergies to things such as house dust mites, mould spores, pollen levels and animal fur. - Irritants in the air such as smoke, air pollution, chemical fumes and cold air. - Respiratory infections such as colds and flu. **Exercise** can cause an asthma attack and is called exercise-induced asthma. Breathing occurs through the mouth during strenuous exercise, which means breathing in air that is colder and drier than usual. Cold, dry air can cause the airways of asthma sufferers to tighten and narrow which can trigger asthma symptoms. The performer will have difficulty getting air into and out of their lungs.	- Wheezing - Coughing - Shortness of breath - Tightness in chest - Pale clammy skin/blue lips - Dizziness/drowsiness/fainting	**Reassurance:** keep the individual calm and provide reassurance as panic can increase the severity of an attack. Encourage them to sit down, loosen clothing and take slow, steady breaths. **Inhalers** are devices for breathing in medicine and help to relieve asthma symptoms when they occur, usually within a few minutes. Inhalers can either help to relieve asthma symptoms (blue reliever inhalers) or prevent symptoms developing (brown preventer inhalers). If the blue inhaler does not relieve symptoms, it is vital to get medical help. **Nebulisers** are machines that allow asthma medicine to be breathed in as a mist through a mask or mouthpiece. They are used for more serious asthma attacks because they can deliver higher doses of asthma medicine quickly and easily. Nebulisers tend to be used by hospitals, GPs and paramedics.

Figure 5.2 Using a nebuliser

> **Typical mistake**
>
> Read the question carefully – sometimes it will give a symptom of a medical condition and ask you to give others. Make sure you do not include the symptom mentioned in the question in your answer.

> **Now test yourself**
>
> A coach suspects a child in an activity session is having an asthma attack. Identify what symptoms the coach should look for.
>
> TESTED

Check your understanding

1. State **three** symptoms of asthma.

5.2 Diabetes

REVISED

Diabetes is a serious medical condition in which blood sugar levels become too high. The carbohydrates we eat and drink are broken down and turned into glucose. This glucose enters the bloodstream and then has to pass into the body's cells where it is broken down to produce energy. Without insulin, the glucose cannot enter the cells so it builds up in the bloodstream and can lead to hyperglycaemia. Sometimes, through excessive exercise or injecting too much insulin, the blood sugar levels of a person with diabetes can drop and they may develop hypoglycaemia (hypos).

5.2.1 Overview of Type 1 and Type 2 diabetes

The differences between Type 1 and Type 2 diabetes in relation to age and lifestyle are as follows:

Age:
+ **Type 1:** most likely to be diagnosed in children and adults up to the age of 40. Most children with diabetes have Type 1.
+ **Type 2:** most likely to get Type 2 diabetes over the age of 40. However, it is currently becoming more common in younger people.

Lifestyle:
+ **Type 1:** thought to be caused by genes and factors in the environment that might trigger the disease. The risk of being diagnosed with Type 1 diabetes is not affected by lifestyle. However, once diagnosed, it is important to lead a healthy lifestyle with regular exercise and a balanced diet to avoid diabetic complications.
+ **Type 2:** eating healthily, doing plenty of exercise and maintaining a healthy weight can all reduce the risk of developing Type 2 diabetes. A family history of diabetes, lack of sleep, stress, smoking and alcohol can all increase the risk of developing Type 2 diabetes.

5.2.2 Causes of Type 1 and Type 2 diabetes

The causes of Type 1 and Type 2 diabetes:
+ **Type 1 diabetes:** where the body's immune system (which normally fights infection) attacks and destroys the cells that produce insulin so that insulin injections have to be taken. This is referred to as insulin-dependent diabetes. People with this type of diabetes need to take insulin every day to stay alive.
+ **Type 2 diabetes:** where the body does not produce enough insulin or the insulin it produces does not work properly. This is referred to as non-insulin-dependent diabetes (or insulin-resistant diabetes) and can be carefully controlled through diet.

5.2.3 Diabetes and exercise

To manage diabetes while taking part in sport it is important to:
+ Check blood glucose levels before and during exercise to work out what should be eaten and when to adjust insulin.
+ Check blood glucose levels regularly after exercise because they can drop up to 12 hours after exercise.
+ Have extra carbohydrates to prevent hypos and drink plenty of water (see links here with dehydration) (Topic area 5.5.9).

> **Exam tip**
>
> Make sure you can explain how to manage asthma when participating in sport/exercise.

> **Diabetes** A lifelong condition that causes blood sugar levels to be too high.
>
> **Glucose** A sugar found in the blood which is a major source of energy.
>
> **Insulin** A hormone made in the pancreas that helps the body to use glucose (sugar) for energy.
>
> **Hyperglycaemia** Occurs when glucose builds up in the blood and blood sugar levels are high.
>
> **Hypoglycaemia (hypos)** Occurs when blood sugar levels are low.
>
> **Insulin-dependent diabetes** Another name for Type 1 diabetes.
>
> **Non-insulin-dependent (or insulin-resistant) diabetes** Another name for Type 2 diabetes.

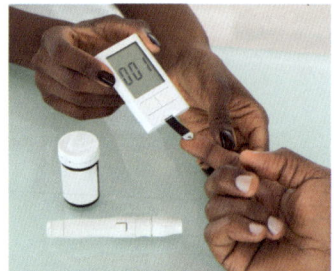

Figure 5.3 Testing for diabetes

Table 5.2 Symptoms, treatment and monitoring of diabetes

Common symptoms of Type 1 and Type 2 diabetes	Treatment of Type 1 and Type 2 diabetes	Monitoring and treatment of different blood sugar levels
<ul><li>Feeling thirsty.</li><li>Increased urination.</li><li>Extreme tiredness.</li><li>Weight loss.</li><li>Cuts/wounds are slow to heal.</li></ul>	**Insulin/glucose**<ul><li>**Type 1 diabetes:** the pancreas no longer makes insulin so it has to be injected to control blood sugar levels.</li><li>**Type 2 diabetes:** the insulin produced by the body does not work well enough. It is possible to control this through a healthy diet and regular physical activity but in some cases it is controlled by medicine to keep blood sugars normal.</li></ul>**Lifestyle changes** Reducing stress and alcohol intake, sleeping well and trying to stop smoking all reduce the risk of developing diabetes. **Diet** It is important for a person with diabetes to maintain a healthy balanced diet and count how many carbohydrates they eat and drink because carbohydrate increases blood sugar levels. They should eat healthy carbohydrates such as wholegrains, starchy foods, vegetables, pulses, nuts and seeds. **Exercise** Exercise helps make the body more sensitive to insulin and helps to control blood sugar levels. It lowers blood pressure and improves good cholesterol (blood fats). Before exercise, it is important to check blood sugar levels and to drink plenty of fluids while taking part.	Individuals with Type 1 diabetes can monitor their blood sugar levels regularly during the day with a finger prick blood test using a flash glucose monitor. Alternatively, they may monitor blood sugar levels through the use of a continuous glucose monitor which is a small device worn just under the skin that sends information to a display using Bluetooth. **Hypoglycaemia (Hypos)**<ul><li>If a participant is suffering from low blood sugar (hypoglycaemia), it can be dangerous if not treated promptly.</li><li>The individual needs to be given fruit juice or sweets.</li></ul>**Hyperglycaemia**<ul><li>If the participant is suffering from high blood sugar (hyperglycaemia), those with Type 1 diabetes have to inject themselves with insulin and those with Type 2 can take medication to lower insulin levels.</li><li>If symptoms do not improve, then it will be necessary to seek medical assistance.</li></ul>

> **Now test yourself** TESTED
>
> Explain how diabetes can be managed during exercise.

> **Check your understanding**
>
> 2 Explain the difference between Type 1 and Type 2 diabetes.

5.3 Epilepsy

REVISED

Epilepsy is a common medical condition that affects the brain and causes seizures. A seizure is a burst of electrical activity in the brain that temporarily affects how it works.

5.3.1 Overview of epilepsy

Epilepsy is a common medical condition occurring when electrical signals in the brain become scrambled and there are sudden bursts of electrical activity which causes seizures. Epilepsy can start at any age but is more common in children and the over 60s. It is usually a lifelong condition but with anti-epileptic medication epilepsy can usually be controlled.

Seizures

A seizure is a burst of electrical activity in the brain that temporarily affects how it works.

5.3.2 Epilepsy and exercise

Individuals with epilepsy can take part in exercise because of the health benefits it brings; it is rarely a trigger for seizures. However, it is important to take precautions with certain activities if seizures are not well controlled. For example, swimming, water sports, skiing and cycling should be avoided unless you are accompanied by another person. Similarly, more dangerous activities such as climbing need to be avoided unless full safety precautions are taken. It is also important to take frequent breaks and drink plenty of fluids and always wear a MedicAlert bracelet or necklace or carry a MedicAlert card.

> **Epilepsy** A medical condition causing abnormal brain activity that leads to seizures.
>
> **Seizure** A burst of electrical activity that temporarily affects how the brain works.

Figure 5.4 MedicAlert bracelet

> **Exam tip**
>
> Questions on epilepsy will ask you to explain how common symptoms of seizures affects the eyes, mouth, arms and legs.

> **Typical mistake**
>
> If a question asks you to give a number, for example, 'Identify **two** …' do not make the mistake of giving more than two answers as the examiner will only mark the first two.

Table 5.3 Common causes/triggers, symptoms and treatment of epilepsy

Common causes/triggers	Common symptoms of seizures affecting parts of the body	Treatment
+ Anxiety/stress is often one of the most common triggers. + Feeling very tired/lack of sleep, which is often a side effect of anti-epileptic medication. + Severe head injury, brain tumour, stroke or a lack of oxygen at birth. + Flashing lights.	The warning signs and general symptoms of seizures affect different parts of the body. + **Limbs:** stiffness and uncontrollable jerking and shaking of the arms and legs. This is called an epileptic fit or seizure. + **Eyes:** losing awareness and staring into space/blankly, blurred vision, eyelids fluttering. + **Mouth:** biting tongue and random noises, often unable to communicate. **Other symptoms can include:** + Collapsing and falling unconscious. + Loss of bladder control. + Breathing problems.	Any person with epilepsy needs to have an emergency care plan in place. + **Treatment for a partial seizure:** when the participant becomes unaware of what is going on around them, keep them safe and calm. + **Treatment for an epileptic fit:** allow the fit to take place and do not hold or restrain the individual. Only move them if they are in danger. Cushion the head if they are on the ground. Any tight clothing around their neck should be loosened. When their convulsions stop, place them into the recovery position. Stay with them and talk to them calmly noting the time the seizure started and finished. + **Call 999 for an ambulance:** if it is the first seizure a person has had, the seizure lasts for more than five minutes, there are lots of seizures in a row, they lose consciousness, the individual has breathing problems or has seriously injured themselves. + **Treatment to control seizures:** can help most people with epilepsy have fewer seizures or stop having them completely. 　+ **Anti-epileptic drugs (AEDs):** help to control seizures. They work by changing the levels of chemicals in the brain. 　+ **Ketogenic diet:** classed as a medical treatment to control seizures. A high-fat, low-carbohydrate diet.

> **Anti-epileptic drugs (AEDs)** Drugs that control seizures by changing the levels of chemicals in the brain.
>
> **Ketogenic diet** High-fat, low-carbohydrate diet.

Now test yourself
TESTED

Identify the body parts affected by epilepsy and explain what happens to them.

Check your understanding

3 In a training session, one of the participants drops to the floor and their body starts to jerk. You suspect they are having a seizure. Describe your response.
4 State a medical condition that requires the following treatments:
　a Treatment: give fruit juice or sweets.
　b Treatment: support or cushion the head.
　c Treatment: give an inhaler.

5.4 Sudden Cardiac Arrest (SCA)

REVISED

Sudden cardiac arrest (SCA) is when the heart stops beating suddenly and without warning due to a problem with the heart's electrical system. As a result, blood flow to the brain and other vital organs stops. Treatment needs to be in the first few minutes to avoid death.

5.4.1 Overview of SCA

SCA is when the heart suddenly stops beating. As a result, oxygen is no longer pumped around the body so the brain is starved of oxygen and this causes you to fall unconscious and stop breathing. A heart attack is different to SCA as this occurs when the blood flow to the heart is blocked.

> **Exam tip**
>
> A sudden cardiac arrest (SCA) is an electrical problem and a heart attack a circulatory problem.

Table 5.4 Causes, symptoms and treatment of SCA

Causes	Symptoms	Treatment
Underlying genetic heart conditions cause an irregular heartbeat, can lead to SCA. **Hypertrophic cardiomyopathy**, for example, is an inherited condition in which the walls of the heart chambers thicken, which affects how well the heart pumps blood around the body. **Intense physical activity** can increase the risk of SCA, mainly because physical activity can sometimes trigger an abnormal heart rhythm. **Sudden trauma** such as a serious chest injury can also cause SCA. Such a trauma directly over the heart at certain points in the heartbeat cycle can sometimes occur in sports with projectiles such as cricket and hockey. This trauma is called **commotion cordis**.	Signs of SCA are instant: + **Unconscious:** the individual collapses and becomes unconscious. + **Breathing difficulties:** discomfort in the chest, no pulse or breathing difficulties. There may also be a fast-beating heart and a feeling of weakness.	Time is critical for a person suffering SCA. When the heart stops, death or permanent brain damage can occur within minutes. **Defibrillators:** it is important to immediately call 999 and find the nearest **defibrillator**. This device comes with voice instructions and when the defibrillator pads are fitted to the chest will check the heart rhythm and give an electric shock to the heart to restart it if needed. However, if a defibrillator is not available, it is important to perform cardiopulmonary resuscitation (CPR) until medical help arrives. **Lifestyle changes:** follow a healthy lifestyle, which includes managing stress, no smoking, regular exercise, healthy diet and not being overweight.

> **Now test yourself** TESTED
>
> Explain what causes a sudden cardiac arrest (SCA).

> **Sudden cardiac arrest (SCA)** A condition in which the heart suddenly and unexpectedly stops beating.
>
> **Genetic** When parents pass some of their characteristics onto their children.
>
> **Hypertrophic cardiomyopathy** A disease in which the heart muscle becomes very thick.
>
> **Defibrillator** A device that sends an electrical impulse/shock to the heart to restore a heartbeat.
>
> **Commotio cordis** A sudden trauma such as a blow to the chest over the heart at certain points in the heartbeat cycle can cause SCA.

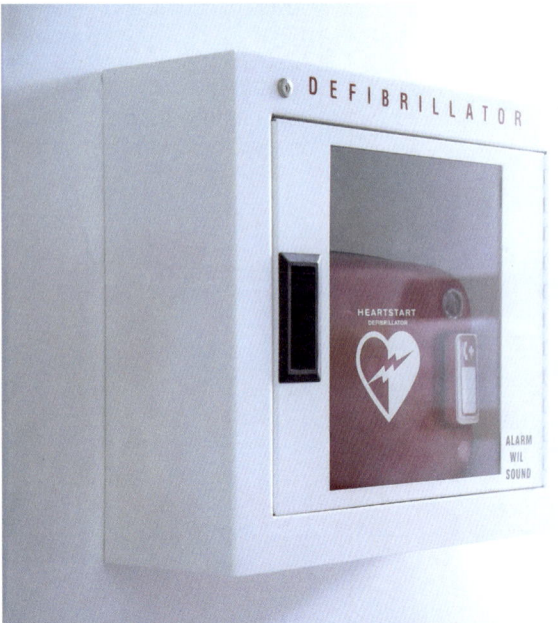

Figure 5.5 Defibrillator

> **Check your understanding**
>
> 5 Describe how you would know whether someone has had a sudden cardiac arrest (SCA).
> 6 A defibrillator is used to treat cardiac arrests. Explain how a defibrillator does this.

> **Exam tip**
>
> Make sure you know the difference between a heart attack and sudden cardiac arrest (SCA).

5.5 Other medical conditions

REVISED

Some medical conditions can happen because it is too hot or too cold.
+ Hot weather means there is an increased risk of dehydration, heat exhaustion and hyperthermia.
+ Cold weather brings the risk of hypothermia.

You need to know the causes, symptoms and treatment of hypothermia, heat exhaustion and dehydration.

> **Dehydration** When the body loses more fluids than it takes in.
>
> **Heat exhaustion** When the body overheats to 38 °C or above.
>
> **Hypothermia** When body temperature drops below 35 °C.

5.5.1 Overview of hypothermia

Hypothermia occurs when the body temperature drops dangerously low. Normal body temperature is around 37 °C and hypothermia occurs as body temperature falls below 35 °C. It is a medical emergency and the person suffering from hypothermia needs to receive hospital treatment.

Table 5.5 Causes, symptoms and treatment of hypothermia

Causes	Symptoms	Treatment
Body temperature drops below 35 °C: caused by exposure to extremely cold conditions. **Prolonged exposure to cold/wet conditions:** this could be a result of not wearing enough sports kit in winter, staying in the cold for too long or clothing being wet.	+ Shivering. + Blue skin and/or lips. + Tiredness/confusion. + Slurred speech. + Slow breathing. + Clumsiness/stumbling.	Hypothermia is a medical emergency which needs urgent treatment in hospital. Until help arrives: + Move the person indoors immediately and make sure someone stays with them. If the person is outside, lay them on a blanket to insulate them from the ground. + Remove any wet clothing and wrap them in something warm such as a blanket and cover their head. + Give them a warm, non-alcoholic drink and some sugary food if they are alert and able to swallow. + Keep them awake by talking to them.

> **Exam tip**
>
> Make sure you also know how hypothermia should **not** be treated. Do not use a hot bath or hot water bottle or rub body parts as this could trigger cardiac arrest.

5.5.2 Overview of heat exhaustion

Heat exhaustion is a medical condition in which the body overheats to 38°C or above. As long as the individual can cool down within 30 minutes it is not serious, but failure to do this can lead to heat stroke, which needs to be treated as an emergency.

> **Heat stroke** When the body is unable to control its temperature and starts to overheat.

Table 5.6 Causes, symptoms and treatment of heat exhaustion

Causes	Symptoms	Treatment
+ Body temperature of 38 °C or above and the person can not cool themselves down quickly enough. High humidity and high temperatures can also increase the risk of heat exhaustion. + Strenuous exercise in hot weather. + Not drinking enough water. It is very important to stay hydrated, especially on hot days.	Symptoms of heat exhaustion can creep up on someone gradually or occur suddenly. + Being very thirsty. + Headache. + Dizziness/confusion. + Fast breathing/pulse. + Excessive sweating. + Pale, clammy skin. + Muscle cramps. + High temperature. + Feeling sick or being sick.	Someone suffering from heat exhaustion should be removed from the heat immediately and allowed to rest. + Move the person to a cool place, preferably indoors or into the shade. + Lie them down and slightly raise their feet. + Give them plenty of water to drink. Sports and rehydration drinks are suitable. + Try to cool the skin with cool water, a fan or cold pack. + Stay with them until they feel better, which is usually within 30 minutes.

5.5.3 Overview of dehydration

Dehydration occurs when the body loses more fluid than is taken in. During exercise, the body will sweat and lose bodily fluids so it is important to drink before, during and after exercise to prevent dehydration (see Topic area 5.2 – diabetes).

> **Fatigue** Extreme tiredness caused by physical exercise.

Table 5.7 Causes, symptoms and treatment of dehydration

Causes	Symptoms	Treatment
Loss of bodily fluids (dehydration): + Dehydration can be caused by exercising in a high temperature of 38°C or more, being in the sun for too long and lots of sweating so the body loses fluids. + Dehydration can also be caused by diabetes, vomiting or diarrhoea.	+ Feeling very thirsty. + Blurred vision/dizzy/light-headed. + Fatigue/tired. + Dry mouth/eyes/lips. + Difficulty chewing, speaking and swallowing. + Dark yellow, strong-smelling urine. + Urinating fewer than four times a day.	+ Drink plenty of fluids. + Consume an oral rehydration sachet (powders containing sugars, salts and minerals) mixed with water. + If symptoms do not improve, go to the accident and emergency department (A&E).

> **Now test yourself** TESTED
>
> Explain how you would recognise dehydration.

> **Check your understanding**
>
> 7 Explain the causes of heat exhaustion.
> 8 State **three** symptoms of hypothermia.
> 9 Describe how you would treat hypothermia while waiting for medical help to arrive.
> 10 Explain dehydration.

> **Exam tip**
>
> Questions could link dehydration to diabetes.

Check your understanding and progress at www.hoddereducation.co.uk/myrevisionnotes

Exam checklist

In 5.1, 5.2, 5.3, 5.4 and 5.5, you learned about the causes, symptoms and treatment of:
+ Asthma.
+ Diabetes.
+ Epilepsy.
+ Sudden cardiac arrest.
+ Hypothermia.
+ Heat exhaustion.
+ Dehydration.

Exam-style questions

1 Identify which of the following is a trigger for epilepsy: [1]

   Choose the correct answer.
   a Dehydration
   b Exercise
   c Fatigue
   d Stress

2 Draw a line to match the following definitions with the medical condition. [3]

Medical condition	Definition
Dehydration	When the body overheats
Heat exhaustion	When body temperature drops below 35 °C
Hypothermia	When the body loses more fluids than it takes in

3 Identify **three** symptoms of diabetes. [3]

4 A treatment for epilepsy is a ketogenic diet. Explain what is meant by the term ketogenic diet. [1]

5 A child in a coaching session is having an asthma attack but they have left their inhaler in the changing rooms. Explain how the coach would deal with the asthma attack until someone arrives with the inhaler. [1]

6 Identify **two** symptoms of hypothermia. [2]

7 State **two** ways in which you would not treat hypothermia. [2]

8 In a tennis session, one of the participants informs the coach that a player on the other court is having a suspected epileptic seizure.
   a Identify **three** parts of the body that the coach could look at to confirm an epileptic seizure. [3]
   b Describe what would be taking place at each body part. [3]

9 It is a very hot day and a football coach suspects that two players are starting to suffer from dehydration.
   a Describe **three** symptoms to look for to confirm that the players have dehydration. [3]
   b State **two** ways in which to treat dehydration. [2]

10 Identify the difference between a heart attack and a sudden cardiac arrest (SCA). [1]

11 If an individual survives a sudden cardiac arrest (SCA), state two ways in which they could improve their lifestyle to prevent it happening again. [2]

12 Complete the table to:
   + Identify **three** symptoms of heat exhaustion.
   + Explain **three** methods of treatment. [6]

Symptom	Treatment
1.	1.
2.	2.
3.	3.

Answers to 'Check your understanding' questions

Topic area 1 Different factors which influence the risk and severity of injury

1. In a contact sport such as rugby, collision in a tackle could cause a dislocated shoulder, and a clash of heads could cause concussion.
2. In a non-contact sport such as gymnastics, a gymnast could sprain an ankle with an awkward landing or strain a muscle in the fast run-up for a vault.
3. An experienced coach can reduce the risk of injury in the following ways:
   + They will have the experience of planning and delivering sports activities in a safe and controlled manner.
   + They can ensure that correct technique is used to reduce the risk of injury.
   + They can provide advice on the correct use of equipment.
4. Poor supervision in a sports session can increase the risk of injury in the following ways:
   + Poor behaviour among participants.
   + Too many performers and not enough supervision.
   + Not watching/observing what the participants are doing.
   + Not enough close supervision in high-risk activities.
5. The playing surface and surrounding area can increase the risk of injury in the following ways:
   + Wet conditions make a playing surface slippery.
   + Very cold conditions can freeze the playing surface, making the ground too hard.
   + The surrounding area may not be clear of any potential equipment that can cause injury.
   + Playing surfaces outside need to be checked for hazards such as glass, wet leaves and dog faeces.
6. Safety checks that an official must do before a sporting activity:
   + Check the playing surface for harmful debris such as wet leaves and glass.
   + Check the area around the pitch for fencing and boards, padding on posts and ensuring corner flags are secure.
   + Check players are wearing suitable clothing and footwear.
7. Equipment can influence the risk of injury in sport in the following ways:
   + An explanation of how not wearing protective equipment can lead to injury with example such as not wearing a gumshield in hockey can lead to injury.
   + Explanation of how performance equipment can lead to injury with example such as a harness in climbing needs to be checked in case it is damaged and will not support the climber.
   + Explanation of how clothing or footwear can lead to injury with example such as not tying up shoelaces on trainers, which results in poor ankle support.
8. Clothing and footwear can lead to injury in sport in the following ways:
   + Loose clothing could catch on something.
   + Warm clothing needs to be worn in cold conditions to keep muscles warm.
   + Footwear needs to be appropriate for the playing surface with example.
9. The age and weight of a performer can increase the risk of injury in the following ways:
   + Older people are less flexible and have less strength so are more prone to injury.
   + Young children need to make sure they do not try to do the same as an adult because they are smaller.
   + Being overweight can damage health and lead to an increased risk of heart disease.
   + Excess weight can lead to stress fractures.
   + Being underweight can lead to fatigue which can cause a lack of concentration and lead to injury.
10. The fitness level of a performer is an important factor in reducing injury for the following reasons:
    + A poor level of cardiovascular fitness results in quicker fatigue and this can lead to injury.
    + Poor strength results in weaker muscles that are quick to fatigue so posture can be affected.
    + Limited flexibility could lead to poor technique and overstretching a muscle.
11. Anxiety can increase the risk of injury in the following ways:
    + Anxiety can make a performer nervous/worried leading to a lack of effort because they fear failing.
    + Reduced concentration/focus.
12. The difference between direct and channelled aggression is as follows:
    Direct aggression involves physical contact with others such as a punch, whereas channelled

Check your understanding and progress at www.hoddereducation.co.uk/myrevisionnotes

aggression is where feelings of aggression are diverted into more positive actions and become controlled and not intended to harm, but injury could still occur, for example, a hard and fair tackle in rugby.

13 The decision of a referee can lead to injuries as a result of:
  + Poor decisions.
  + Belief that a referee is not being fair.

14 The difference between mental rehearsal and imagery is as follows:
  Mental rehearsal is when a performer goes over the movements of a task in their mind before the action takes place, whereas imagery is where a performer pictures a successful performance in their head to reduce stress.

Topic area 2 Warm-up and cool down routines

1 Examples of activities for each component of a warm-up include:
  + Pulse raising – light jogging/cycling.
  + Skill rehearsal – any skill-based drill such as shooting/passing.

2 The benefits of the components of a warm-up are as follows:
  + Pulse raising – increases heart rate/raises muscle temperature.
  + Mobility – increases the range of motion.
  + Dynamic stretching – increases range of motion/flexibility/makes tendons and ligaments more flexible.
  + Skill rehearsal – prepares the body for techniques/skills and improves reaction/response time and confidence.

3 The psychological benefits of a warm-up can help to avoid injury in the following ways:
  + An example to show how mental rehearsal improves focus/concentration – for example, a gymnast who does a potentially dangerous activity, such as the beam, could use imagery to practise movements that improve concentration and focus to help avoid injury.
  + An example to show the importance of controlling arousal – for example, a football player might control their anxiety and therefore be less likely to perform dangerous tackles.

4 The physical benefits of a warm-up can help a performer avoid injury in the following ways:
  + Increase in muscle temperature which results in greater flexibility/mobility/increases range of motion.
  + Increases heart rate, resulting in an increase in blood flow and oxygen to the working muscles, which delays fatigue.
  + Increase in pliability (of ligaments and tendons).
  + More force can be applied due to an increase in the speed of muscle contraction, which helps reduce injury.

5 Three types of stretching that can be used in a cool down are as follows:
  + Static stretches.
  + Maintenance stretches.
  + Proprioceptive neuromuscular facilitation (PNF) stretching.

6 Light running:
  + gradually lowers the heart rate
  + circulates blood and oxygen
  + gradually reduces the breathing rate.

7 Stretching:
  + removes waste products such as lactic acid from the muscles
  + reduces the risk of delayed onset of muscle soreness (DOMS)
  + prevents blood pooling in the muscles
  + returns the muscles used in the session back to their normal length.

Topic area 3 Different types and causes of sports injuries

1 A sprain is an injury to ligaments and a strain is an injury to muscles and tendons.

2 Sprain and strains can be caused in sport in the following ways:
  + Sprain – a twisting/turning example or excessive force example where the muscle is stretched too far.
  + Strain – an example of an excessive stretch that causes a tear/a change of speed/a high intensity example/overuse.

3 The ACL is located in the middle of the knee.

4 A bruise which is caused by damaged blood vessels. Examples include contact with the ground in a fall or contact with another performer.

5 Blisters can be caused by poorly fitting footwear that causes friction or by the use of sports equipment such as a racket. Blisters can be treated by cleaning, sterilising and applying a dressing if necessary.

6 The difference between an open and closed fracture is:
   + An open fracture is where the bone is broken and breaks the skin.
   + A closed fracture is where the bone is broken but there is no break in the skin.
7 Examples of contact sports where blows to the head can take place are football, rugby and boxing.
8 + A chronic injury results in immediate pain. **False**
   + A chronic injury occurs over a long period of time. **True**
   + An open fracture is an example of a chronic injury. **False**
9 The difference between an acute and chronic injury:
   + An acute injury is caused by a sudden trauma and pain is felt immediately. Examples include strains of muscles and tendons, ligament sprains, skin damage injuries such as abrasions, cuts, contusions and blisters, open, closed and stress fractures, dislocations and head injuries.
   + A chronic injury is caused by overuse. Examples include tendonitis (Achilles, rotator cuff and patellar), tennis elbow, golfer's elbow and shin splints.
10 Shin splints is a chronic injury. Treatment for shin splints includes rest, applying ice, and taking pain and anti-inflammatory medication.
11 A runner can reduce the risk of a stress fracture by warming up properly, stretching thoroughly and applying ice after training and rest.

Topic area 4 Reducing risk, treatment and rehabilitation of sports injuries and medical conditions

1 It is important to carry out a risk assessment for a sporting activity to reduce the chances of injuries occurring by making equipment, the performer and the performance area safe.
2 The supervisor should check:
   + the playing surface for harmful debris such as glass
   + the area around the pitch for fencing and boards, ensuring that there is padding on posts and that corner flags are secure
   + players for suitable clothing, footwear, jewellery and loose hair.
3 The three main components of an EAP are:
   + emergency personnel
   + emergency communication
   + emergency equipment.
   Examples:
   + Emergency personnel – any one of the following: first responder, qualified first aider, coach, doctor/nurse.
   + Emergency communication – dial 999 and ask for an ambulance.
   + Emergency equipment – any one of the following: first aid kit, evacuation chair, wheelchair, stretcher, defibrillator, inhaler and ice packs.
4 The stage of the SALTAPS on-field assessment routine that the statements explain are:
   + Checking for bleeding, bruising, swelling or deformity – look.
   + Examining the injured area for pain and tenderness – touch.
5 The difference between 'active' and 'passive' for the on-field assessment of SALTAPS is as follows:
   + Active is where the performer tries to move an injured area themselves.
   + Passive is where the first aider tries to move the injured area.
6 You would apply the PRICE procedure for an injury over two to three days.
7 Massage can help in the treatment of sports injuries:
   + Increases blood flow.
   + Increases flexibility.
   + Relaxes/loosens muscle.
   + Relieves pain/manages DOMS.
   Splints can help in the treatment of sports injuries:
   + Keep an area of the body held in a comfortable position.
   + Keep an injury still/supported.
   + Prevent further injury.
   + Elevate injury/to reduce swelling or raise above heart.
8 Any two from:
   + heat pads
   + deep heat cream
   + hot water bottles
   + heat lamps
   + massage
   + hot bath.
9 Any two from:
   + Improves blood circulation.
   + Relieves pain.
   + Relaxes muscles.
   + Supports body weight.
   + Strengthens the injured area.
10 Cryotherapy is the use of cold temperatures to treat an injury.

Check your understanding and progress at www.hoddereducation.co.uk/myrevisionnotes

Topic area 5 Causes, symptoms and treatment of medical conditions

1 Three symptoms of asthma:
   + Wheezing.
   + Coughing.
   + Shortness of breath.
   + Tightness in chest.
   + Pale clammy skin/blue lips.
   + Dizziness/drowsiness/fainting.
2 The difference between Type 1 and Type 2 diabetes:
   + Type 1 is where the body's immune system attacks and destroys the cells that produce insulin.
   + Type 2 is where the body does not produce enough insulin or the insulin it produces does not work properly.
3 Response to someone having a seizure:
   + Allow the fit/seizure to take place and do not hold or restrain the individual.
   + Only move them if they are in danger.
   + Cushion the head if they are on the ground.
   + Loosen tight clothing around the neck.
   + When their convulsions stop, place them into the recovery position.
   + Stay with the participant and talk to them calmly, noting the time the seizure starts and finishes.
4 a Diabetes.
   b Epilepsy.
   c Asthma.
5 Evidence of an SCA:
   + The individual collapses and becomes unconscious.
   + There is no pulse or breathing.
6 A defibrillator is a device that sends an electrical impulse/shock to the heart to restore a heartbeat.
7 The causes of heat exhaustion:
   + Body temperature of 38°C or above.
   + Strenuous physical activity.
   + Not enough water intake.
8 Symptoms of hypothermia:
   + Shivering blue lips/skin.
   + Slurred speech.
   + Tiredness/confusion.
   + Slow breathing.
9 Treatment of hypothermia while waiting for medical help to arrive:
   + Move the person indoors immediately and make sure someone stays with them.
   + Remove any wet clothing and wrap them in something warm like a blanket and cover their head.
   + Give them a warm, non-alcoholic drink and some sugary food.
   + Keep them awake by talking to them.
10 Dehydration occurs when the body loses more fluid than is taken in.

Answers to exam-style questions

Topic area 1 Different factors which influence the risk and severity of injury

1 Three marks from three of:
   + Activities can be contact and non-contact.
   + Example of one contact activity and one non-contact activity.
   Examples of injuries that could occur with a justification:
   + Contact activities will tend to have injuries caused by impact.
   + Non-contact sports could have muscle sprains or strains from twisting.
   + Some sports such as tennis have repeated actions so the performer could end up with an overuse injury.

2 Three marks from three of:
   + Explanation of how knowledge of techniques/rules/regulations leads to injury with example.
   + Explanation of how lack of experience leads to injury with example.
   + Explanation of how poor communication skills lead to injury with example.
   + Explanation of how lack of supervision leads to injury with example.
   + Explanation of how poor ethical standards or behaviour leads to injury with example.

3 Three marks from three of:
   + Explanation of how weather can lead to injury with example.
   + Explanation of how a poor playing surface or surrounding area can lead to injury with example.
   + Explanation of how human interaction from either participants/officials/spectators can lead to injury with example.

4 Four marks from four of:
   + Gender.
   + Age.
   + Experience.
   + Weight.
   + Fitness levels.
   + Technique/ability.
   + Nutrition.
   + Sleep.
   + Previous/recurring injuries.
   + Hydration.
   + Medical conditions.

5 One mark for:
   d Experience.

6 One mark for a type of performance equipment from:
   + Bat.
   + Ball.
   One mark for a type of protective equipment from:
   + Helmet.
   + Pads.
   + Box.
   + Gloves.

7 Three marks for three of:
   + Type of sports activity/contact/non-contact.
   + Coaching/instructing/leading.
   + Environment.
   + Equipment.

8 Two marks:
   + Too much aggression can lead to a lack of control.
   + Negatively affects technique.

9 Two marks from two of:
   + Prevents muscle recovery, making muscles more susceptible to injury.
   + Leads to fatigue/reduces concentration levels (with a suitable example of how this can cause injury, such as collisions with other players).
   + Makes an individual irritable and aggressive (with a suitable example of how this can cause injury, such as dangerous tackles).

10 Two marks from two of:
   + Risk of collisions.
   + Foul play due to a lack of knowledge of the rules.
   + Too aggressive/over competitive/being silly.
   + Inappropriate equipment/footwear/long nails/wearing jewellery/long hair not tied back.

11 Two marks:
   + An increase in motivation increases drive and could lead to recklessness with an example (such as contesting for a ball could result in injury).
   + Over-arousal may result in the performer being too reckless/overly aggressive with an example (such as a dangerous football tackle).

12 Possible content:
   + Contact sports – football/boxing/rugby and any other relevant example.
   + **Factor: type of activity**
   + Explanation:
      + Contact sports present different injury risks from non-contact activities, for example, impact injuries such as concussion in a tackle.

Check your understanding and progress at www.hoddereducation.co.uk/myrevisionnotes

- Factor: coaching/supervision
- Explanation:
  - Incorrect coaching techniques, for example, a player not using correct technique in a tackle, such as the head in the incorrect position.
  - Poor communication skills from the coach, for example, not able to hear the coach.
  - Not adhering to rules and regulations, for example, two-footed tackles in football.
  - Experience of the coach, for example, a new coach may make mistakes with instructions leading to dangerous play.
  - Ethical standards and behaviour, for example, encouraging foul play.
- Factor: environmental factors
- Explanation:
  - How weather can lead to injury, for example, icy pitch.
  - How a poor playing surface or surrounding area can lead to injury, for example, a boggy pitch can cause injury when the foot sticks in the mud and the body twists.
  - How other performers can lead to injury, for example, players pushing another player/collisions.
  - How spectators can lead to injury, for example, encouraging unfair play.
- Factor: equipment
- Explanation:
  - Protective equipment – how not wearing protective equipment can lead to injury, for example, scrum hat/mouth guard/shoulder pads/boxing gloves/shin pads.
  - How performance equipment can lead to injury, for example, not wearing shin pads.
  - How footwear can lead to injury, for example, incorrect studs.

Topic area 2 Warm-up and cool down routines

1. One mark for each answer:
   - Pulse raising.
   - Skill rehearsal.
2. One mark for each answer:
   - Mobility – arm/leg swings.
   - Dynamic stretching – change of speed/direction.
3. One mark for each answer – maximum of three marks:
   - Heightens or controls arousal levels.
   - Improves concentration and focus.
   - Increases motivation.
   - Increases confidence.
   - Time when mental rehearsal can take place.
4. One mark for each answer – maximum of three marks:
   - Increase in muscle temperature.
   - Increase in heart rate.
   - Increase in flexibility of muscles and joints.
   - Increase in pliability of ligaments and tendons.
   - Increase in blood flow and oxygen to muscles.
   - Increase in the speed of muscle contraction.
5. One mark for each answer:

Cool down component	Practical example	Explanation
Pulse lowering	Light running or walking.	Gradually lowers heart rate, temperature and breathing rate/prevents blood pooling.
Maintenance stretching	Stretching example, e.g. shoulder/hamstring/quadriceps stretch.	Reduces lactic acid build-up/reduces the risk of delayed onset of muscle soreness (DOMS).

6. One mark for each answer – maximum of three marks:
   - Gradually reduces heart rate.
   - Gradually lowers temperature.
   - Gradually reduces breathing rate.
   - Helps prevent blood pooling.
   - Removes waste products such as lactic acid.
   - Reduces the risk of delayed onset of muscle soreness (DOMS).

Topic area 3 Different types and causes of sports injuries

1. One mark for each answer:

Injury type	Chronic or acute
Tendonitis	Chronic
Concussion	Acute
Ankle sprain	Acute
Abrasion	Acute

2. One mark for each answer – maximum of two marks:
   - A twisting example such as landing and twisting to face the direction of the next pass.
   - A quick change in direction that takes place when running.

My Revision Notes Cambridge National Level 1/Level 2 in Sport Science Second Edition

- Stopping suddenly such as running in one direction and then stopping to dodge an opponent to get free.
- Overextending the knee on landing.
- A collision takes place where there is a direct blow to the knee.

3 One mark for each answer – maximum of three marks:
- Tendonitis (Achilles/rotator cuff/patellar).
- Shin splints.
- Tennis elbow.
- Golfer's elbow.

4 One mark for each:

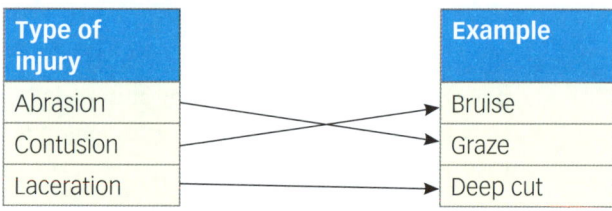

Type of injury	Example
Abrasion	Bruise
Contusion	Graze
Laceration	Deep cut

5 One mark for each type of injury – maximum of three marks:
- Patellar tendonitis.
- ACL strain.
- Muscle sprain.
- Abrasion.
- Cut/laceration.
- Contusion.
- Dislocation.

6 One mark for each:

	Cause	Treatment
Muscle strain	• Physical contact occurs with others, for example, a tackle in football causing ankle ligament damage. • Landing incorrectly, for example, a poor landing after a vault in gymnastics or from an attempted interception in basketball. • Twisting, for example, a netball player turning and twisting as they land to face the direction of their next pass, resulting in a muscle strain or ligament sprain. • Falling, for example, tripping over another player's foot, causing a sprain.	splint/sling/call 999 or medical assistance/put in plaster/cast.
Concussion	hard impact to head (by a piece of sports equipment/another player/with the ground).	apply ice/rest or medical assistance or call 999.

7 One mark for an explanation of tendonitis – inflammation or irritation of a tendon.
One mark for each symptom – maximum of two marks:
- Joint pain.
- Mild swelling.
- Thickness of the tendon.
- Tenderness and stiffness which limits the range of motion.

8 One mark for any of the following:
- Continuous or repetitive use of the arm/shoulder when swimming or bowling in cricket or serving in tennis or completing lots of passes in netball/basketball/rugby
- or other relevant practical example involving the shoulder.

9 One mark for head injury.

10 One mark for:
a elbow.

11 One mark for each answer – maximum of three marks:
- Do not overload too quickly.
- Poor technique and training.
- Wearing incorrect equipment and clothing/worn-out trainers.
- Poor core stability/lack of muscle strength/lack of endurance.
- Muscle imbalance/strong tight muscles/lack of flexibility.
- Biomechanical issues/flat-footed.

12 One mark for each:
- An open fracture is when the soft tissue or skin has been damaged because the bone has moved or broken through the skin.
- A closed fracture is a clean break to a bone that does not penetrate through the skin or damage any surrounding tissue.

One mark for each cause – maximum of four marks:
- Physical contact with others, for example, a tackle in football.
- Being hit with sporting equipment, for example, a hockey stick.
- Landing incorrectly, for example, a poor landing after a vault in gymnastics or from an attempted interception in basketball.
- Twisting, for example, a netball player turning and twisting as they land to face the direction of their next pass.
- Falling, for example, tripping over another player's foot.
- Collisions with sporting equipment, for example, a goalkeeper in football making contact with the post in an attempt to save a shot.

Check your understanding and progress at www.hoddereducation.co.uk/myrevisionnotes

Topic area 4 Reducing risk, treatment and rehabilitation of sports injuries and medical conditions

1. One mark for either of the following:
   + Check the playing surface for harmful debris such as wet leaves and glass.
   + Checking the area around the court for fencing/boards/padding on posts.
2. One mark for each of the following – maximum of two marks:
   + Age of the group.
   + Size of the group.
   + Individual fitness levels.
   + Experience of the group.
   + Any medical conditions such as asthma or diabetes.
3. One mark for each correctly drawn line.

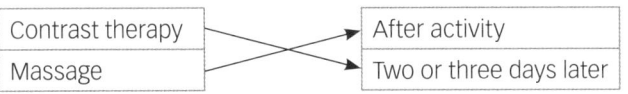

4. One mark for each answer:
   + **Look** at the injury site for bruising, bleeding, swelling or deformity.
   + **Touch** the area gently to feel for swelling, deformity, heat, lumps or bumps.
5. One mark for each answer:
   + R = response
   + B = breathing
6. One mark for unconscious player who is breathing.
7. One mark for each of the following – maximum of two marks:
   + Reduce blood flow to the injured area.
   + Reduce swelling.
   + Ease pain.
8. One mark each for two of the following – maximum of two marks:
   + Risk of infection.
   + Heavy blood loss.
   + Where it could make pain worse by applying it.
9. One mark for any of the following – maximum of two marks:
   + Prevents swelling.
   + Prevents bleeding.
   + Prevents infection.
   + Provides support.
   + Holds an ice pack in place.
10. One mark for:
    c Hydrotherapy.
11. Your answer should include:
    + Explanation of the different treatment/therapies.
    + Examples of sporting injuries.
    + How each treatment/therapy can rehabilitate the injury.
    + **Explanation of the different treatment/therapies:**
      - **Massage:** use of hands or massage guns to rub and knead muscles and joints.
      - **Ultrasound:** a medical test that uses high-frequency sound waves to create a live image of the injury inside your body.
      - **Electrotherapy:** the application of an electric current to the injury.
      - **Hydrotherapy:** the use of water in the treatment of injuries.
      - **Cryotherapy:** the use of cold temperatures to treat an injury.
      - **Contrast therapy:** the use of alternating hot and cold temperatures.
      - **Painkillers:** medication that reduces pain such as Ibuprofen – an anti-inflammatory drug that also relieves pain.
      - **Kinesiology tape:** a tape that provides support.
      - **Neoprene:** a synthetic rubber material that supports an injury.
      - **Bandaging:** use of a protective strip of material on an injury.
      - **Cast:** a stiff bandage.
      - **Splint:** a hard piece of medical equipment.
      - **Sling:** a piece of material that supports and immobilises an injury.
    + **Injury examples for each method:**
      - **Massage:** soft tissue injuries such as a muscle strain/ligament sprain/chronic injuries.
      - **Ultrasound:** can be used to diagnose any injury. But often used for more serious injuries such as an ACL rupture.
      - **Electrotherapy:** used for most soft tissue injuries and chronic injuries to soft tissue.
      - **Hydrotherapy:** often used for stress fractures in the feet or lower leg but can be used for most soft and hard tissue injuries and chronic injuries.
      - **Cryotherapy:** an injury such as a sprain/bruising and most chronic injuries or example of a chronic injury.
      - **Contrast therapy:** an injury such as a sprain, strain, bruising and most chronic injuries or example of a chronic injury.
      - **Painkillers:** can be used for any injury as pain is always experienced.
      - **Kinesiology tape:** tends to be used for muscle strains and ligament sprains.
      - **Neoprene:** used for muscle strains and ligament sprains.
      - **Bandaging:** cuts/lacerations/blisters/abrasions.
      - **Cast:** used for more serious injuries such as fractures/Achilles tendon tears.
      - **Splint:** used for fractures/dislocations.
      - **Sling:** used for fractures/dislocations.

- How each treatment/therapy rehabilitates the injury:
  - Massage:
    - Improves circulation by increasing blood flow, which moves fluid and nutrients through damaged tissue, encouraging healing and accelerating the removal of waste products.
    - Scar tissue is broken down, helping muscles to relax; relieves tension.
    - It can also be used to manage pain and relieve DOMS (delayed onset of muscle soreness).
  - **Ultrasound:** this allows a medical professional to assess the damage and decide how to treat the injury.
  - **Electrotherapy:** accelerates healing and reduces swelling and pain.
  - **Hydrotherapy:** improves blood circulation, relieves pain and relaxes muscles. The buoyancy of the water helps to support body weight.
  - **Cryotherapy:** lowers pain and can limit swelling by causing vasoconstriction of blood vessels, decreasing blood flow to the injured area.
  - **Contrast therapy:** increases blood flow and decreases swelling and pain after exercise. Should only take place several days after the injury has happened.
  - **Painkillers:** reduce pain and swelling.
  - **Kinesiology tape:** provides support and keeps muscles and joints in place to reduce mobility, therefore reducing pain.
  - **Neoprene:** supports an injury and provides compression.
  - Bandaging:
    - Prevents swelling by reducing blood flow to the injured area.
    - For abrasions and blisters, it can stop bleeding and prevent infection.
    - Can also be used for support or to hold an ice pack in place.
  - **Cast:** immobilises and protects the injured site and holds the injury in place, keeping it secure. Relieves pain and reduces stress around the injured part.
  - Splint:
    - Immobilises and protects the injured site and holds the injury in place, keeping it secure. Relieves pain and reduces stress around the injured part.
    - Can be used to elevate the injury to reduce swelling.
  - Sling:
    - Immobilises and protects the injured site and holds the injury in place, keeping it secure. Relieves pain and reduces stress around the injured part.
    - Can be used to elevate the injury to reduce swelling.

Topic area 5 Causes, symptoms and treatment of medical conditions

1 One mark for
   d Stress.
2 One mark for each correctly drawn line – maximum of three marks:

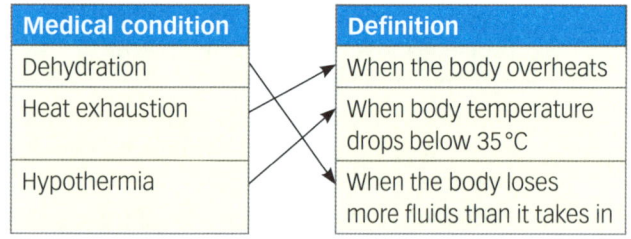

3 One mark for each of the following – maximum of three marks:
   + Feeling thirsty.
   + Increased urination.
   + Extreme tiredness.
   + Weight loss.
   + Cuts/wounds that heal slowly.
4 One mark for: high-fat, low-carbohydrate diet.
5 One mark for: reassure and keep calm.
6 One mark for each symptom – maximum of two marks:
   + Shivering.
   + Blue skin and/or lips.
   + Tiredness/confusion.
   + Slurred speech.
   + Slow breathing.
   + Clumsiness/stumbling.
7 One mark for each of the following – maximum of two marks:
   + Do not use a hot bath or hot water bottle.
   + Do not rub body parts.
8 a One mark for each – maximum of three marks:
     + Eyes.
     + Mouth.
     + Limbs/arms and legs.
   b One mark for each – maximum of three marks:
     + Eyes – staring blankly into space/losing awareness/eyelids fluttering/blurred vision.
     + Mouth – biting tongue/making random noises/often unable to communicate.
     + Limbs – stiffness/jerking movements.

9 a One mark for each – maximum of three marks:
- Feeling thirsty.
- Tired.
- Dark yellow urine.
- Infrequent urination.
- Dry mouth/lips/eyes.

b One mark for each – maximum of two marks:
- Drink plenty of water.
- Rehydration sachets.

10 One mark for identifying the difference as:
- A sudden cardiac arrest (SCA) occurs when the heart suddenly stops beating and a heart attack occurs when the blood flow to the heart is blocked.

11 One mark for each – maximum of two marks:
- No smoking.
- Regular exercise.
- Healthy diet.
- Not being overweight.

12 One mark for each symptom (maximum of three marks) and one mark for each treatment method (maximum of three marks):

Symptom	Treatment
- Being very thirsty. - Headache. - Dizziness/confusion. - Fast breathing/pulse. - Excessive sweating. - Pale, clammy skin. - Muscle cramps. - High temperature. - Feeling sick or being sick.	- Move the person to a cool place, preferably indoors or into the shade. - Lie them down and slightly raise their feet. - Give them plenty of water to drink. Sports and rehydration drinks are suitable. - Try to cool the skin with cool water, a fan or cold pack. - Stay with them until they feel better, which is usually within 30 minutes.

My Revision Notes Cambridge National Level 1/Level 2 in Sport Science Second Edition

Glossary

Abrasion Where the surface of the skin is damaged. 36

Achilles tendon Found at the back of the ankle and connects the calf muscle to the heel bone. 40

Acute injury Caused by sudden trauma where pain is felt immediately. 33

Aggression Forceful action caused by feelings of hostility or anger, which can cause harm to others. 22

Alzheimer's disease A type of progressive and irreversible form of dementia that affects memory, thinking and behaviour. 38

Analgesic A medicine that relieves pain. 53

Anterior cruciate ligament (ACL) The ligament that runs diagonally in the middle of the knee joining the femur to the tibia in the leg. 35

Anti-epileptic drugs (AEDs) Drugs that control seizures by changing the levels of chemicals in the brain. 61

Anti-inflammatory medication Medicine that reduces swelling. 37

Anxiety When a performer experiences worry, nervousness and apprehension. 22

Arousal The level of body and mind stimulation that gets us ready to perform. 22

Asthma A lung condition in which the airways narrow and swell, which can make breathing difficult. 20, 56

Bandaging A protective strip of material on an injury. 53

Blisters Small fluid sacks that are caused by friction. 36

Carbohydrates Nutrients that should form the main source of energy. 20

Cardiorespiratory system Consists of the heart and blood vessels which work together with the lungs in the respiratory system. Together they transport oxygen to the muscles and organs of the body. 28

Cardiovascular fitness The ability of the body to take in and use oxygen while exercising. 20

Cast A stiff bandage to immobilise and protect an injury. 53

Channelled aggression When feelings of aggression are diverted into positive, productive actions. 23

Chronic injuries Overuse injuries caused by repetitive movement that places stress on a particular muscle, tendon, ligament, bone or joint. 39

Circulation Where the heart pumps blood around the body. 49

Closed fracture Where a bone is broken but there is no break in the skin. 37

Commotio cordis A sudden trauma such as a blow to the chest over the heart at certain points in the heartbeat cycle can cause SCA. 62

Concussion An injury that occurs when the brain is shaken inside the skull. 37

Contact sport A sport in which there is physical contact between performers. 11

Contrast therapy Alternating hot and cold temperatures. 53

Contusion A bruise caused by blood leaking into the area. 36

Cool down Easy exercises that are performed after more intense activities in order for the body to gradually move to a resting condition. 29

CRY An abbreviation for 'cardiac risk in the young'. 47

Cryotherapy The use of cold temperatures to treat an injury. 53

Cut/laceration Where the skin tears. 36

Defibrillator A device that sends an electrical impulse/shock to the heart to restore a heartbeat. 62

Dehydration Occurs when the body loses more fluid than is taken in, leading to headaches, dizziness and feeling tired. 15, 63

Delayed onset of muscle soreness (DOMS) A muscle pain that occurs 24–48 hours after a strenuous exercise session. 31

Dementia A general term for a decline in mental ability, which affects the ability to perform everyday activities. 38

Diabetes A lifelong condition in which blood sugar levels are not regulated by the body effectively. 20, 58

Direct aggression Involves physical contact with others. 22

Dislocation Where the bones in a joint become separated. 37

DOMS (delayed onset of muscle soreness) Acronym for delayed onset of muscle soreness. Muscles are sore 24–48 hours after exercise. 52

DRABC An acronym for the steps that should be followed when initially attending to an injury: Danger, Response, Airway, Breathing and Circulation. 49

Dynamic stretches Moving stretches that increase the range of motion of a joint. 26

ECG Stands for an electrocardiogram machine. Electrodes are placed onto the player's chest and the wires connect to an ECG machine and a printout is produced of the heart's electrical activity. 47

Check your understanding and progress at www.hoddereducation.co.uk/myrevisionnotes

Electrotherapy The application of an electric current to the injury to accelerate healing and reduce pain and swelling. 53

Emergency action plan (EAP) A written plan detailing what action and procedures need to be followed in the event of an emergency. 47

Endorphins Chemicals produced naturally by the nervous system to help us cope with pain and stress and that boost happiness. 54

Epicondyles A part that sticks out at the end of a bone where tendons and ligaments attach. 41

Epicondylitis A painful swelling of tendons at the end of a bone. 41

Epilepsy A medical condition causing abnormal brain activity that leads to seizures. 60

Extrinsic factors Risk or factor that causes an injury that comes from outside the body. 11

Fatigue A feeling of overwhelming tiredness caused by physical exercise. 19, 64

Fractures The medical term for broken bones. 34

Gastrocnemius The main calf muscle. 30

Genetic When parents pass some of their characteristics onto their children. 62

Glucose A sugar found in the blood which is a major source of energy. 58

Golfer's elbow (medial epicondylitis) Inflamed tendons that cause pain around the inside of the elbow. 42

Hamstrings A group of muscles located in the back of the thigh. 30

Hard tissue injuries Injuries to the skeletal system such as fractures or dislocations. 33

Hazards An unsafe condition that can cause injury. 45

Heat exhaustion When the body overheats to 38 °C or above. Occurs as a result of prolonged exposure to excessive or unaccustomed heat, leading to fatigue and collapse. 15, 63

Heat stroke Occurs when the body fails to regulate temperature, leading to fever and unconsciousness. 15, 64

Hydrotherapy The use of water in the treatment of injuries. 53

Hyperglycaemia Occurs when glucose builds up in the blood and blood sugar levels are high. 21, 58

Hyperthermia Occurs when an athlete's body temperature rises and remains above the normal temperature of 37 °C (98.6 °F). 20

Hypertrophic cardiomyopathy A disease in which the heart muscle becomes very thick. 62

Hypoglycaemia (hypos) Occurs when blood sugar levels are low. 21, 58

Hypothermia When body temperature drops below 35 °C. Occurs when the body temperature drops dangerously low, leading to shivering, slurred speech and tiredness. 15, 63

Ibuprofen An anti-inflammatory drug that also relieves pain. 53

Imagery Enables a performer to picture a successful performance in their head to reduce stress. 24

Immobilisation Keeping the injury still. 53

Inhaler A device that allows medicine to be breathed in to relieve asthma symptoms. 56

Insulin A hormone made in the pancreas that helps the body to use glucose (sugar) for energy. 58

Insulin-dependent diabetes Another name for Type 1 diabetes. 58

Intrinsic factors A risk or factor that causes an injury that comes from inside the body. 19

Isometric contraction Where a muscle is contracting but there is no movement. 30

Joint Where two or more bones meet. 37

Ketogenic diet High-fat, low-carbohydrate diet. 61

Kinesiology tape Tape that provides support and keeps muscles and joints in place to reduce mobility, therefore reducing pain. 53

Lactic acid Waste product of anaerobic exercise; causes fatigue. 31

Ligaments Fibrous tissue that connects bone to bone and strengthens joints. 21, 28, 34

Maintenance stretching For muscles that are already flexible, aiming to maintain the range of movement. 30

Massage Using hands or massage guns to rub and knead muscles and joints to relieve pain and tension. 52

Medicals An examination by a doctor to assess a person's physical health and fitness. 47

Mental rehearsal When a performer goes over the movements of a task in the mind before the action takes place. 24

Minerals and vitamins Substances needed for many essential functions of the body. 20

Mobility Swinging exercises to increase the range of motion. 26

Motivation A person's drive to succeed. 21

Musculoskeletal system Includes bones, cartilage, ligaments, tendons and connective tissues. 28

Nebuliser A machine that allows high doses of asthma medicine to be breathed in as a mist through a facemask or mouthpiece. 57

Glossary

Neoprene A synthetic rubber material that supports and compresses an injury. 53

Non-contact sport A sport in which players are kept apart and any physical contact is penalised, for example, in netball the umpire will award a penalty pass. 12

Non-insulin-dependent (or insulin-resistant) diabetes Another name for Type 2 diabetes. 58

Open fracture Where a bone is broken and breaks through the skin. 37

Oxygenated Arterial blood (in arteries) that carries oxygen. 26

Painkillers Medication that reduces pain. 53

Patellar tendon Found at the knee and connects the kneecap (patella) to the shin bone (tibia). 40

PRICE An acronym for a treatment method for acute soft tissue injuries, in which the letters mean protection, rest, ice, compression and elevation. 34, 50

Proprioceptive neuromuscular facilitation (PNF) A progressive stretch involving muscle contraction and relaxation. 30

Pulse raising An activity that increases heart rate. 26

Recovery position A position used to keep an airway clear and open in an unconscious patient. 50

Retaliation The act of harming someone because they have harmed you. 23

Risk A possibility of injury. 45

Risk assessment Identifies the possible hazards or risks that can cause injury and how to avoid them. 45

Rotator cuff tendons A group of tendons that attach the shoulder muscles to the upper arm (humerus). 40

SALTAPS An acronym for the steps that should be followed to assess the seriousness of an injury: See, Ask, Look, Touch, Active movement, Passive movement and Strength testing. 49

Screening Identifies the current medical condition of an individual to determine whether there is a risk of complications from exercise. 47

Seizure A burst of electrical activity that temporarily affects how the brain works. 60

Selective attention Filtering out irrelevant information. 24

Shin splints (medial tibial stress syndrome) Pain along the shin bone (tibia) caused by exercise. 42

Skill rehearsal Practising common movements and skills. 26

Sling A piece of material that supports and immobilises an injury. 54

Soft tissue injuries Injuries to muscles, tendons, ligaments and skin. 33

Splint A hard piece of medical equipment that protects and immobilises an injury. 53

Sprains Injuries to ligaments. 34

Static stretching Involves holding a stretch for 30 seconds to improve flexibility. 30

Strains Injuries to muscles. 34

Strategy A plan of action. 47

Stress A person's reaction to feeling threatened or under pressure. 22

Stress fracture A very small crack in a bone caused by overuse or repetitive force. 20, 43

Sudden cardiac arrest (SCA) A condition in which the heart suddenly and unexpectedly stops beating. 62

Sudden trauma An impact that happens very quickly and causes an acute injury. 33

Support Something that keeps a joint in place. 53

Technique Method used to perform a skill. 12

Tendon Joins muscle to bone. 28, 34

Tendonitis Inflammation or irritation of a tendon. 13, 40

Tennis elbow (lateral epicondylitis) Inflamed tendons that cause pain around the outside of the elbow due to repetitive actions such as tennis strokes. 12, 41

Triggers Things that make the onset of a medical condition more likely. 57

Ultrasound A medical test that uses high-frequency sound waves to create a live image of the injury inside your body. 53

Vasoconstriction The narrowing of a blood vessel to reduce blood flow. 53

Vasodilation The widening of a blood vessel to increase blood flow. 53

Warm-up Exercises to prepare the body for exercise so that the chances of injury or ill effects are reduced. 26

X-ray Uses images to see where a bone is fractured or dislocated. 51

Check your understanding and progress at www.hoddereducation.co.uk/myrevisionnotes